The Jew and His History

Scholars Press
Reprints and Translations Series

Published through the cooperation and support of the American Academy of Religion, the Society of Biblical Literature, the American Society of Papyrologists, the American Philological Association, and Brown Judaic Studies.

The Jew
and His History

Lionel Kochan

Scholars Press
Chico, California

The Jew and His History

Lionel Kochan

First published by Schocken Books, 1977

Scholars Press Reprint, 1985

Reprinted by permission of The Macmillan Press

© Lionel Kochan, 1977

Library of Congress Cataloging in Publication Data

Kochan, Lionel.
  The Jew and his history.

  (Scholars Press reprints and translations series)
  Reprint. Originally published: New York : Schocken
Books, 1977.
  Bibliography: p.
  Includes index.
  1. Jews—History—Philosophy. 2. Historians, Jewish.
I. Title. II. Series.
DS115.5.K62   1985   909'.04924   84–27587
ISBN 0–89130–821–0 (alk. paper)

Printed in the United States of America
on acid-free paper

To Miriam :

Grow old along with me
The best is yet to be.

Robert Browning,
Rabbi Ben Ezra

To enlighten the Jewish nation we must begin neither with history nor with natural theology and morals. One of my reasons for thinking so is that these subjects, being easily intelligible, would not instil any regard for science into the more learned Jews, who are accustomed to respect only those studies which involve a strain upon the highest intellectual powers.

Solomon Maimon, *Autobiography*

In general we utterly neglect historical research.

Kafka, *Josephine the singer, or the mouse-people*

Contents

Introduction
to the Scholars Press Reprint

The reprint of this book gives me a most welcome opportunity to reconsider in brief, after a lapse of almost a decade, my earlier thinking on the subject of Jewish historical writing.

This took as its starting point the virtual absence of any Jewish historiographical tradition, save for the tradition of legal history, following the work of Josephus.[1] The present bloom of historical study, both in Israel and the Diaspora, only throws into greater relief the dearth that characterises the past. It is with the period of cultural and intellectual transition that I would have wished to have occupied myself in greater detail. But at this stage I will limit myself to a few further words, in an attempt merely to indicate the problem.

How is the movement from penury to plethora to be accounted for? What must be explained is not only a change in the consciousness of time; in addition, and inseparably so, a change in the evaluation of the past *tel quel*.[2] As to the first, the one-dimensional vision which does not distinguish between past and present is displaced by the awareness of a plurality of dimensions; as to the second, the newly created past forfeits its capacity to

---

[1] Cf. also Y. H. Yerushalmi, *Zakhor*, Washington University Press, 1982, pp. 16ff., and the same author's 'Clio and the Jews', *Proceedings of the American Academy for Jewish Research*, vols. xlvi–xlvii, ed. S. W. Baron and I. E. Barzilay, Jerusalem, 1980, pp. 613ff.

[2] See now Ismar Schorsch, 'The Emergence of Historical Consciousness in Modern Judaism', *Leo Baeck Year Book*, xxviii, 1983, pp. 413–37; also R. Paine, 'Israel and Totemic Time?,' *Royal Anthropological Institute News*, No. 59, December 1983, pp. 19–22. (I am indebted to Dr. Jonathan Webber for drawing my attention to this article.)

serve as a fount of instruction or to be studied for its normative content but becomes a medium of instruction in its own right. The two stages seem to be encapsulated and to fall at some point in the latter part of the eighteenth century. When the proposal is mooted in the Mendelssohn circle in Berlin, whereby a Hebrew translation of Basnage's history of the Jews becomes a vehicle for the enlightenment of Eastern European Jewry,[3] then not only is some sort of sea-change in Jewish historical consciousness in the making—some sort of caesura in the awareness of the passage of time—but the plurality of teachings and their particular Sitz im Leben stands revealed. The consequence was soon underlined by Zunz, in the early nineteenth century, in his programme of Jewish scholarship: 'our science,' he wrote, 'is to emancipate itself from the theologians and rise to the historical viewpoint . . . ; we are not afraid of being misunderstood. Here the whole literature of the Jews, in its widest context, is presented as an object for research, without our being concerned whether its total content also should or can be a norm for our own judgement.'[4] But if, in the twelfth century, it was possible for Maimonides to assimilate Greek and Arabic notions of philosophy and at the same time to reject alien notions of historiography, why, in the nineteenth century, was this no longer possible for Zunz? Mendelssohn, of the previous generation, had displayed a certain aversion to historical concerns. His successors, such as Zunz and the school of the Wissenschaft des Judentums, had no comparable reluctance. Indeed, critical historiography was their forte.

---

[3] See below, p. 64.

[4] Quoted below, p. 66; cf. also L. Wieseltier, 'Etwas über die jüdische Historik: Leopold Zunz and the Inception of Modern Jewish Historiography', *History and Theory*, xx, no. 2, 1981. This detachment, alienation even, from the notion of norm is echoed, a century and a half later, by the Israeli historian Scholem: 'I do not hold to the opinion of those . . . who view the events of Jewish history from a fixed dogmatic standpoint and who know exactly whether some phenomenon or another is "Jewish" or not. Nor am I a follower of that school which proceeds on the assumption that there is a well-defined and unvarying "essence" of Judaism, especially not where the evaluation of historical events is concerned. . . . There is no way of telling a priori what beliefs are possible or impossible within the framework of Judaism. . . . The "Jewishness" in the religiosity of any particular period is not measured by dogmatic criteria that are unrelated to actual historical circumstances' (G. Scholem, *Sabbatai Sevi: The Mystical Messiah*, Eng. trans., London, 1973, pp. xi, 283).

The explanation, it would seem, is to be sought less in the notion of intellectual influence or attraction, but rather in the changing social and political status of the Jew in certain parts of Germany. It proved undesirable, perhaps even impossible, to participate in the work of the Christian world, to attend Christian universities, and not simultaneously to assimilate Christian ways of thought. The discussion of Jewish autonomy in Prussia and Alsace in the 1770s and 1780s already presaged a closer rapprochement between Jewish and Christian society.[5] This development of course also drew reinforcement from the theory of a voluntary Jewish community as propounded in Mendelssohn's *Jerusalem*: 'Seen in the context of his concern for civil admission, this powerful advocacy of a totally non-coercive type of religion appears as the final effort on Mendelssohn's part to facilitate the integration of the Jews into the secular state.'[6] There is certainly a connection between this process, however limited it was at the outset, and the flowering of historical study.

But the consequence was in large measure to weaken, perhaps even to remove, the normative qualities of the material studied. Into the quasi-vacuum thus created there flowed varied attempts to salvage the past. In their contrapuntal approaches, for example, both Krochmal and Rosenzweig sought to mediate between the new thinking and the old, i.e., to accept and also to master the challenge presented by a world devoid of norms. The former devised a system of historical cycles in which all manifestations of Judaism in their appropriate sequence could claim legitimacy; the latter altogether removed the Jews and Judaism from history by positing an ideal, eternal realm of law where the Jew led an existence impervious to time.

This too proved a failure. The challenge remains: the tree of knowledge of good and evil has been found sweet to the taste. How is this to be combined with a reversion to the past as a source of instruction?

[5] Cf. F. Malino, 'Attitudes Towards Jewish Communal Autonomy in Pre-Revolutionary France', *Essays in Modern Jewish History*, ed. F. Malino and P. C. Albert, London-Toronto, 1982, pp. 95–117.

[6] A. Altmann, 'Philosophical Roots of Mendelssohn's Plea for Emancipation', *Essays in Jewish Intellectual History*, New Hampshire-London, 1981, p. 163.

Preface

This book began life as an attempt to examine the course of Jewish historiography in the Diaspora. But the more that subject matter came to be known, the more it dwindled. The original enquiry then set itself the further question : why did the historical dog not bark more loudly? When it did, what special factors governed its expression?

The answer proffered here draws on the works of historians as well as others who have not written a line of history and would be astonished, and perhaps also repelled, to find themselves described as historians. But this is inherent in the subject, for those 'others' have yet propounded distinctive notions of Israel's past and future. 'History is important to such a degree', it has been said, 'that even values beyond space and time are not alienated from it but relate to it in a positive manner'.[1] Not only does messianic thinking and exposition associate itself with particular historical events but its point of reference is also historical in that it encompasses the political and physical destiny of Israel.[2]

This must necessarily be so. The idea of the messiah is here understood as that concept which encompasses all those other concepts – the election of Israel, the covenant with God, the *Torah* – which have history as their 'all-pervading dominant sanction'.[3] For this reason Jewish historiography cannot exist as an historical discipline or enquiry independent of Judaism, however understood; it can only seek to express the changing manner in which the messianic theme has been understood. But this definition is in itself already so wide that every mystic, for example, who has reflected on the fact and meaning of exile should be regarded as an historian. It is natural that a study entitled 'Different Approaches to the History of Israel'[4] should consider the mystical teaching of R. Isaac Luria, with its doctrine of the restoration of all things

A*

to their primal source in God, side by side with the sociological doctrines of Dubnow. Faced with this profusion of matter, and its indeterminacy, I have arbitrarily tended to limit myself to those historians who favoured an empirical approach.

This has inevitably posed problems of selection, and means that this book can make not the slightest claim to comprehensiveness. Given this limitation, however, I would like to think that the essay will expound an understanding of history drawn from the thinking of exilic Judaism.

To my dear friend Steven Schwarzschild I owe a debt of gratitude which I hope this essay may in part redeem. His stimulating conversation and correspondence greatly helped me in the clarification of my ideas.

To the Overseas Research Fund of the University of Warwick, which helped to make it possible for me to consult colleagues and libraries in Israel, I am also deeply grateful.

University of Warwick   LIONEL KOCHAN

1 The Problem

'Within the whole gate of my people (Ruth III, 11) there has not yet arisen an historian in Israel like Josephus . . . they ceased, the writers of memorials, they ceased, until I arose, even I, Joseph' (Judges v, 7). In these words, R. Joseph Ha'Cohen (1496–1578), the author of a history of the kings of France and Ottoman Turkey, signified the novelty of his enterprise. His contemporary, R. Solomon Ibn Verga, seems to confirm this notion of Jewish unconcern with the past and to make it a source of reproach. In his chronicle of persecution, *Shevet Yehudah* (Adrianople, 1553), Ibn Verga seems to suggest a contrast, unfavourable to the Jews, between *their* attitude to history and that of the Christians. At one point, when he is relating the downfall of Persia in its war with Ishmael (Islam), allegedly because of the persecution it had inflicted on the Jews, Ibn Verga expresses the hope that the King of Spain will benefit from this precedent, when it is brought before him, 'as is the custom of the Christians, for they will wish to know earlier matters to take counsel from them and this is because of their insight and their enlightenment'.[1]

Is it in fact true of the millenium and a half separating Josephus from Joseph Ha'Cohen that 'the writers of memorials' ceased in Israel? The answer is 'yes', much qualified.

Not until the eighteenth to nineteenth century did certain Jewish scholars feel this as a keen reproach. In the 1820s and after, for example, when Isaac Marcus Jost (1793–1860) came to write his histories of the Jews he complained bitterly that his sources contained 'almost nothing but the sequence of the transmission of rabbinic teachings, the martyrologies of the Jews, now and again with reference to outside events but these [are] absolutely devoid of sources . . . Chronology and knowledge of places are everywhere confused . . . So far as regards historical works all we have in recent times is a miserable, very unreliable chronicle by David Gans . . .' Jost excepted from these strictures some accounts of specific experiences (e.g. Usque's 'Consolacam', 1553) and a multitude of reports of specific events and biographical or autobiographical narratives.[2] Another scholar of the nineteenth century, R. Solomon Judah Rappoport, in his study of R. Nathan b. Yehiel (one of the heads of the *Yeshivah* in Rome in the second half of the eleventh century) spoke of the 'reproach [expressed] by non-Jewish scholars who mock us, saying there is no exactitude and no truth in the narratives of the times of the great ones of Israel . . .'[3]

Much of Rappoport's work was devoted to removing this very reproach. A similar motive animated R. Nahman Krochmal (1785–1840) from whom it ultimately evoked a major philosophy of Jewish history. He too aimed to overcome the historical apathy and ignorance of his contemporaries. In general terms, Krochmal's aim was 'to make peace between reason and the two *Torahs*, to reveal the root and the source of matters that the peoples of the world and the frivolous-minded of our own community scornfully argue are beyond understanding'.[4] He saw enemies on several fronts. On the religious, for example, he felt compelled to take up arms against *Schwärmerei, Aberglauben* and *Werkheiligkeit* – enthusiasm, superstition and salvation by works alone. These Krochmal saw as various forms of sickness of the soul or deficiencies of the intellect.[5] Other enemies were those who feared and hid the truth : 'we will say and repeat it yet many times that in the same way as the danger in earlier generations was to reveal the concealed, then even more so the danger in our own generation is to conceal what has already been revealed by others, a vain and noxious activity in which there is no help at all.'[6]

Krochmal, as a counter-principle of elucidation, used the results of historical research, no matter whether they emanated from Jewish or non-Jewish scholars (and he was himself influenced by the German Biblical scholar Eichorn), 'to interpret and to examine and to establish each matter in relation to its appropriate time of composition'. A psalm, for example, that refers to 'the waters of Babylon' should no longer enjoy its traditional Davidic attribution by way of divine vision; however valuable this attribution may have been in the past, today 'the contrary' applies and the psalm should rather be attributed to a Levite exiled from the Temple.[7] Thus Krochmal gave special attention to the history of the Jewish calendar, 'for the most urgent and useful thing in relation to all sequence of the generations and historical narrations, following each other in time, is a fixed calendar, clear and accepted by all.'[8]

By such means Krochmal hoped to silence 'the sceptics, the challengers, the scoffers'; he would respond to the needs of his own generation for 'a refined faith', attained through the exercise of reason, and thus follow in the footsteps of Maimonides, confronted by a generation no less perplexed than the contemporaries of Krochmal.[9] Such an achievement would also entitle Israel to take its due place amongst the enlightened nations of Europe.[10]

The self-criticism generated by this apparent historical unconcern was simultaneously accompanied by a search for its cause. When scholars of the late eighteenth and nineteenth centuries turned to this topic they were quasi-unanimous in attributing the phenomenon to the absence of a Jewish political entity. Since the defeat of the Jewish state at the hands of the Romans, there was no longer any Jewish history and therefore no historians. At the end of the eighteenth century, for example, the philosopher Solomon Maimon wrote : 'There is no proper history of the Jewish nation for they have scarcely ever stood in any political relation to other civilised nations, and, with the exception of the Old Testament and Josephus and a few fragments on the persecution of the Jews in the Middle Ages, nothing is to be found on the subject.[11] A half century or so later, Zunz wrote : 'If the Jewish Middle Ages can show no historians or historical researchers we should not be surprised. A nation *in partibus* performs no acts . . . Scientific awareness, even the need for historical research was lacking.' Israel's history 'was brought to an end' with the collapse of the Jewish state . . .[12]

In the heyday of nationalism it would indeed be natural for a nation without a state not to be considered fully historical, to exist in some sort of ahistorical limbo. This would be all the more so at a time when the unit of historical study was predominantly the state. On both counts the Jews in the nineteenth century could be likened to the non-historic nations (Rumanians, Bulgarians, Ukrainians, etc.) as distinct from the historic nations (Hungary, Germany, Italy, etc.). The work of Moses Hess straddled both positions and added a religious dimension. He attributed the supposed absence of Jewish history to the rejection of Jesus. In a remarkable image, strong with Toynbeean overtones, Hess compared the Jews to a 'mummy', through their rejection of Jesus.[13] In his later argument Hess succumbed to his time when he claimed that only if the Zionist prince-charming awoke the Jews to the resumption of their own national life in the land of Israel could their history, suspended for two thousand years, begin afresh. The non-historical would become historical. The Jewish sleeping beauty, no longer a 'mummy', would be restored to the land of the living, that of the European nations : 'The Jewish people, which has not in vain defied for two millenia the storms of world history . . . and from all the ends of the earth has never ceased to look to Jerusalem, belongs unquestionably to the peoples believed dead which in the consciousness of their historical task must assert their national rights.'[14] (It is indeed characteristic of the alienated Jew – e.g. Spinoza and Marx – to transfer the impetus for preservation from the Jew to society; the former declaring in his *Theologico-Political Treatise* that the Jews 'have been preserved in great measure by gentile hatred'; the latter in his *On the Jewish Question* that 'Judaism has been preserved not in spite of history, but by history'.)

Les extrêmes se touchent. Hess the nationalist was joined by Holdheim, the liberal and radical critic of Jewish tradition, who argued that under the dominion of the rabbis the Jews had been brought into conflict with the world of time and life.[15]

An explanation along these lines, couched in political terms, in terms of Jewish statelessness, does not however do justice to the Jewish position. A problem does indeed revolve around the unit of Jewish history. It was not the least of Dubnow's merits, for example, that he sought to overcome the problem by treating Jewish history in terms of communities.[16] But to make the problem into a solution and to put forward the mere absence of a state as an explanation for the apparent lack of historical interest is a criterion drawn not from the Jewish world but rather from the Christian, from that world which had normally – and at no time more than in the nineteenth century – conceived of the state as *par excellence* the unit of historical writing. By this criterion the Jewish experience must *eo ipso* fall short.

At another, and related, level of misunderstanding, not only did the Christian world share the view of those Jewish thinkers who argued that Israel had no history in the Diaspora because it had no state, but also, from the traditional and representative Christian standpoint, Judaism, after the destruction of the Jewish state, now existed in a sort of limbo. Judaism, as a preparation for Christianity, had been superseded, so that no further Jewish existence could belong to history proper. A survey of Christian writings about Jews yields this result:

> before the first century A.D. the Hebrews were of great historical importance; thereafter the Jews are of little significance. The reign of a new truth had begun. So deep are the roots of identity that historians whose religion, if any, is well concealed (e.g. Voltaire, Gibbon) have remained faithful to this element of Christian historiography even when they have abandoned the Christian account of Christianity . . . After the emergence of Christianity, a reprobation falls on the Jews, and a dark night of ignorance conceals their activities from the historical consciousness of most of Western society until Dreyfus, the Balfour Declaration, or Hitler once more draws attention to the Jews.[17]

In a more kindly vein there is Weber's presentation of what he understood as the system of late-rabbinic, pharisaic law in terms of a means to preserve its adherents from participation in the life of the peoples. The Talmud's 'four cubits of the law', and the rabbinic tradition that grew from it, delineated a framework that persuaded Weber to articulate the notion of a Jewish communal existence in terms of 'a self-chosen situation as pariah-people'.[18] It had deliberately renounced the world of history and limited itself to a life within the confines of late-rabbinic law, in the conviction that the existing order was provisional and must yield to a just order that would restore to the Jews their true place. Weber wrote with no pejorative intent, and the Jewish posture that he saw commanded his admiration. But in the lecture, *Wissenschaft als Beruf*, delivered to the students of Munich University in 1918, Weber revealed the limits of his understanding. He quoted: 'One calleth unto me out of Seir: "watchman, what of the night? watchman, what of the night?" The watchman said: "The morning cometh, and also the night – if ye will enquire, enquire ye; return, come." ' (Isaiah xxi, 11–12) Weber continued: 'The people to whom this was said has enquired and tarried for more than two millenia, and we are shaken by its fate.' Nothing was to be gained 'by yearning and tarrying alone, and we shall act differently', Weber concluded.[19] In recent years, Toynbee has rationalised and secularised the Christian view and made of the Jews 'a fossil people'.[20]

Even if the modern Jewish and the Christian world are at one, albeit for reasons that sometimes differ and sometimes tally, in arguing that the mantle of Clio rests uneasily on the Jews, the phenomenon has still to be examined in the light of its origins, from the 'inside', as it were. It is important and rewarding not to bring to Judaism a question beyond and outside its terms of reference, but to expound the notion of its history in terms that do justice to its own inherent preoccupations. Did the Jews look on themselves as a 'fossil' or as a self-enclosed 'pariah-people', indifferent to the turbulence of world history, sheltering within the walls of a timeless rabbinic law? On the contrary, the Jews saw themselves as the very axis of world history. What will be argued here is that it is a misnomer to suggest that Jewish historical awareness atrophied through the condition of statelessness, though this did indeed affect that awareness. Rather, it developed a character *sui generis* whereby the ever-changing present is comprehended and expressed and mastered through reference to a past that includes, moreover, a means also to shape the future.

2 The Affirmation of History

Rosenzweig has recently argued that those who live by the Law, because the Law is unchanged and unchanging, are removed from 'all the temporality and historicity of life'.[1] But this fails to take account of the flexibility of the Law and its ability to adapt itself to ever novel circumstances. To take the Jews from the world and the life of history and to transport them to a point beyond history, to a meta-historical location, assuredly challenges the customary association between Judaism and the world.

It is a basic rabbinic dictum that 'the world and its fullness were only created for the sake of the *Torah*'.[2] Indeed, R. Abbahu argued that of all the worlds that God had created and destroyed, this particular cosmos gave Him particular pleasure.[3] Therefore, should Israel have rejected the *Torah* – and its acceptance, according to certain Talmudic teachers, only took place under extreme duress – then, argued Resh Lakish, the world would have reverted to its primeval state of formlessness.[4] In short, without Israel, there would be no world and therefore no history. To the Jew the historical world must be of supreme importance as that domain in which the relationship of Israel and God is being played out, i.e. that domain in which Israel's obligations *vis-à-vis* the *Torah* are to be fulfilled. Present here is a historical God who, in the words of the liturgy, 'remembers the pious deeds of the patriarchs and brings a redeemer to their children's children.' He binds together the past and the future.[5] The covenant concluded in the desert encompassed the unborn generations of the future as much as those actually present. 'Neither with you only do I make this covenant and this oath; but with him that standeth here with us this day before the Lord our God, and also with him that is not here with us this day' (Deuteronomy xxix, 13, 14). History is a record of divine revelation so that a knowledge of God and the understanding of history are inseparable.[6]

The validity of a positive affirmation of the historical process was early tested and elaborated in the Talmud. The sages had to confront the capture of Jerusalem by the Romans in 70, the failure of the Bar-Kochba revolt against Rome and the fall of Betar in 155. These cataclysmic events inevitably determined the attitude of the Tannaitic teachers to the past and present.[7] On the one hand, there was a revulsion against the contemporary world and contemporary history. God Himself was shown to be estranged from this world of Israel's suffering: 'Woe to the children on account of whose sins I have destroyed My house, burnt My temple and exiled them amongst the peoples of the world.'[8]

But for all the intensity of the estrangement, there was no renunciation of the world as such, no negation of the world, no search for refuge in eschatological or apocalyptic visions. Lack of confidence in history or of a positive attitude to the world was tantamount to a lack of trust in God. In the name of R. Meir an interpretation of Jacob's dream was propounded in which Jacob saw the princes (or guardian angels) of Babylon, Persia, Greece and Rome, rise and descend. But when Jacob was told by God to ascend he feared to do so, in case he, in his turn, also fell. Thereupon, said R. Meir, God told Jacob 'because you did not trust and did not go up, your children will be subjugated to the four kingdoms in this world.'[9]

A prerequisite of confidence in God was the closest possible identification with the historical past. In this context, of outstanding importance is the vehemence with which the scriptural documents demand to be recalled:

> take heed unto yourselves, lest ye forget the Covenant of the Lord your God . . . for ask now of the days past, which were before thee, since the day that God created man upon the earth, and from the one end of heaven unto the other, whether there hath been any such thing, as this great thing is, or hath been heard like it? . . . Thou shalt remember well what the Lord thy God did unto Pharoah, and unto all Egypt . . . Remember the days of old, consider the years of many generations . . . Remember the former things of old: that I am God and there is none else; I am God and there is none like Me; Declaring the end from the beginning, and from ancient times things that are not yet done.[10]

Indeed, the Talmud turned attachment to the past into identification with the past : 'In every generation a man is bound to regard himself as though he personally had gone forth from Egypt, because it is said, and thou shalt tell thy son in that day saying : it is because of that which the Lord did for me when I came forth out of Egypt' (quoting Exodus XIII, 8).[11]

This provided the motive-power and substance of an additional memory, as it were, apart from the personal, in which the phenomenon of total recall of the remote past co-existed with relative oblivion to the recent past. Lestchinsky has seen this in terms of 'two trends in Jewish life . . . on the one hand a remarkable collective memory stretching across two thousand years, and on the other a tendency to forget recent experiences, a complete blank in regard to what has happened in the Diaspora over a few generations.'[12] This latter phenomenon was already noted in Talmudic times. R. Joseph, for example, compared Israel to a man who met a wolf from which he escaped; he carried on his way narrating the affair of the wolf; then he met a lion, again he escaped, but the lion replaced the wolf in his narration; then he met a snake, which in turn replaced the lion : 'so it is with Israel – the later troubles make them forget the earlier ones.'[13] But by virtue of what Lestchinsky calls 'the long memory', the Jew of the Diaspora is at one with his past.

The process of identification was the precondition for what has been termed 'the activation of history'.[14] Given that this is still God's world, even though contemporary affairs are almost too painful to contemplate – then, if confidence in the divine plan is at this time to be preserved, recourse must be had to that earlier time when God's presence and activity were unmistakeably manifest, i.e. *par excellence the* Exodus from Egypt and the wandering in the desert. The historical world retained all its importance as that dimension of man's existence where the divine purpose has been revealed and where it will be fulfilled.[15] The past – history – became more important than ever, as a source of models, solace and promise. This enabled the generations of the stateless and the dispersed to see themselves in the perspective of history and to draw comfort from the trials that, with God's help, they had successfully overcome. R. Nathan told of a king whose bride only reached him after a hazardous sea voyage. He told her not to remember the waves but rather the day she was saved from them. 'Israel likewise : The Holy One Blessed be He was revealed to them to their Saviour, and how many heavy waves passed over them but He brought them to salvation.'[16] There is here a corresponding understanding of the present as an epoch of danger, to be viewed, however, in terms of future deliverance. The past was activated on such a scale that it replaced the actual contemporary world and served as a source of encouragement.[17] The scriptural period of manifest divine intervention was, as it were, called in to redress the balance of that later period when divine intervention seemed no longer to be manifest. The present had to be validated through the past, which was thereby imbued with a contemporary bearing and relevance.

This process had enormous manifestations and consequences. It eliminated, for one thing, the possibility that a historically neutral area might exist. The Talmudic teachers knew of no area not subject to an historical interpretation, conceived in terms of present trends, and thereby grasp, for everything not in the historical realm was unreal. So strong indeed was the affirmation of history that it transformed the non-historical into the historical. R. Akiba (2nd century), for example, invested a passage from the Songs of Songs ('Go thy way forth by the footsteps of the flock', i, 8) with a meaning that brought it into the historical realm by attaching it to the relationship between God and Israel.[18] Another example of a non-historical text applied to a historical situation was the identification by R. Akiba's pupil, R. José b. Halafta, of 'the wild beast of the reeds' (Psalms LXVIII, 51) with Rome.[19] Similarly, R. Judah Hanassi interpreted 'The righteous and the wicked God will judge' (Ecclesiastes III, 17) as meaning : 'God judges a righteous man through a wicked man' and then applied this abstract dictum to the contemporary world : 'Thus Tineius Rufus judged R. Akiba'.[20] This technique could also be used to make sense of the catastrophe in terms of human guilt and thus salvage even that catastrophe as part of the continuing schema of redemption. It could be argued, for example, that the fall of Betar and the death of the Jewish leader Bar-Kochba were due to his killing of R. Eleazar of Modim.[21] Similarly, R. Simon b. Yochai, commenting on Jeremiah IX, 11 ('Wherefore is the land perished and laid waste like a wilderness . . .?') attributed this to the fact that the scribes and teachers had not been rewarded.[22]

But perhaps the most impressive use of the technique of 'activating' the past – i.e. of seeing the present through the past, of transposing the past into the present – was to make the past contain within itself the promise of future triumph over the Romans. R. Akiba, for example, came to Mount Scopus with some companions and saw a fox emerging from the Holy of Holies. But by bringing together prophecies from Isaiah and Zechariah, Akiba was able to visualise the fulfilment of Zechariah's prophecy: 'Thus saith the Lord of Hosts, there shall yet old men and old women sit in the broad places of Jerusalem' (vIII, 4).[23] In the same way R. Nehamia found confidence in the ultimate defeat of Rome by identifying those 'adversaries' and 'enemies' on whom God would take revenge (Isaiah I, 24) with the Four Kingdoms, of which Rome was the last, following Babylon, Persia and Greece.[24]

If, now, the question is asked: why did Israel not interest itself in its history, despite the historical nature of its God, the answer is – precisely *because of* that God's historical nature. The record of His doings and promises as narrated in the Hebrew scriptures, and appropriately understood, utterly exhausted all putative historical interest. The affirmation of history, embodied in those scriptures, removed all need to study history, for in themselves the scriptures answered all historical questions – where Israel originated, where it stands and where it is going. R. Saadya Gaon, the tenth-century philosopher of Egypt and Babylon, could therefore see the whole history of Israel in the song of Moses (*Ha'azinu*, Deuteronomy xxxII):

> it begins with our first election by God and says, 'remember the days of old, consider the years of many generations' . . . then secondly the song mentions, 'He found him in a desert land'. Third, it mentions our prosperity and sins, saying, 'but Jeshurun waxed fat and wicked'. Fourth, it mentions our punishment and says, 'and God saw and spurned . . .' Fifth, comes the punishment of our enemies, saying, 'for their wine is of the wine of Sodom'. Then, sixth, it speaks of our redemption and salvation, from the verse, 'see now that I, even I, am He, and there is no god with me.'[25]

This makes for an instructive comparison, sociologically speaking, with the Christian world; if the history of the Jew has already been written, that of the Christian requires perpetual renewal.

If it is true to say that Judaism was able to generate a sense of identity and historical location amongst its adherents, then it would presumably follow that Christianity, its role as a universal religion making it impossible to give a common sense of identity to its varied adherents, would find it necessary to have recourse to history.

But precisely what history? The resultant confusion is beautifully expressed in Hegel's early work *The Positivity of the Christian Religion* (1799–1800). It is true that this was a peculiarly sensitive epoch for German thinkers. Even so, Hegel's description of the German predicament can easily be generalised. Christianity 'has depopulated Valhalla, cut down the sacred groves', he argues. What has it replaced them with? The imagery of a nation whose laws, culture and so on are 'alien' to us. A David or a Solomon live in the popular imagination, whereas 'the heroes of our fatherland slumber in the history books of scholars.' The memory of the heroes of the Reformation likewise 'slumbered in us . . .' As for the Greeks – 'is then Achaea the Teutons' fatherland?' Hegel asked rhetorically, and again he asked, 'is then Judea the Teutons' fatherland?'[26] It is true of course that the Israelites too had once 'served other gods' (Joshua xxiv, 2) and more than once relapsed into their former ways (as for example in the episode of the golden calf). But these were overcome and were followed by the successful assimilation and retention of a new historico-religious affiliation.

If therefore the 'long memory' of the would-be Jewish historian already contains within itself the recollection of the divine promise to Israel, the burden of the Exile, the knowledge of the uniqueness and centrality of Israel, together with the certainty of ultimate redemption – then, is not his historical framework predetermined? Is not his 'present' diminished to the point of eclipse? Must he not also realise that his history is in fact already written? The revelation at Sinai, for example, already promises Israel a part of central importance in the world's future in that, through Israel, 'shall all the families of the earth be blessed' (Genesis xii, 5). Israel already knows its end – whatever tribulations the Exile may bring, whatever disappointments lie ahead, it is part of the very order of the world that Israel will enjoy the messianic reward. Of the ultimate success of Israel's efforts there can be no doubt. The would-be historian can never say anything that will remotely rank in importance with the content of that 'long memory'. Again, if the historian's models belong to the past, if his identification with the past is as complete as Scripture and the Talmud sought to make it, it is difficult to see how any other historical interest could ever arise. If the *Torah* already contains the most important truths – then, clearly, no possibility of further meaningful history can exist. No subsequent events can conceivably add to what has already been made manifest. It is possible to go even further and to maintain that, strictly speaking, no further historiography is necessary. The contents of the 'long memory' refer not only to origins and beginnings and identity but also to future and finality. It answers all questions that can conceivably be asked of any historian. What Freud called the *Diesseitigung der Lebensauffassung* – the world grasped as a here-and-now[27] – in itself averts the sentiment of alienation and quest for identity that are otherwise essential components of the historiographical urge.

But this still leaves open the question of the future. Here indeed was the crux of the prophetic influence on the concept of history. Far from considering prophetic teaching to be involved with contemporary iniquities or political circumstances (e.g. Isaiah's warning to the Kingdom of Judah against concluding an alliance with Egypt), it is more rewarding in the present context to note its reference to the future and more particularly its historiographical bearing. The concept of present time is diminished by the reference to the future. In this sense the prophets, as Hermann Cohen pointed out, 'created the concept of history as the essence of the future'. 'Through the ideal significance of the messiah time becomes future and only future. Past and present are submerged in this time of the future'.[28]

When R. Akiba, for example, his eyes sharpened by the words of Isaiah and Zechariah, perceived the future restoration of the Temple, he thereby established a model for later historical writing. The primordial fact about the present world is that it exists in an incomplete state, awaiting (perhaps actually undergoing) completion and perfection. Perhaps indeed there are already signs that the process is in motion :

Everything that the Holy One Blessed be He will do and make anew in the world to come – all that He has already performed in part in this world through His prophets, and the Holy One Blessed be He said: 'I am He who will one day make the sea dry. Have I not already done so through Moses, as it is written: And lift thou up thy rod [Exodus XIV, 16]? I am He who will take thought for the childless. I have already done so, as it is written, 'And the Lord remembered Sarah' [Genesis XXI, 1]. I am He who will bring it about that kings bow down to you, as it is written, 'And kings shall be thy foster-fathers, And their queens thy nursing mothers' [Isaiah XLIX, 25]. I have already done this through Daniel, for 'Nebuchadnezzar fell upon his face and worshipped Daniel' [Daniel II, 46].[29]

In any case, only this future-directed process can excite historical interest. History is conceived as a process of messianic redemption. 'God works salvation in the midst of the earth' (Psalms LXXIV, 12), and the task of the historian is to elucidate this process of salvation. Whether redemption would be cataclysmic or gradual, whether it lay entirely in God's hands or could be hastened (or retarded) by the actions of man – here opinions differed. Here, 'each generation has its interpreters' but that redemption formed part and parcel of the structure of the universe – that it was indeed the very purpose of the universe – here all 'interpreters' were in agreement. It was the task of the historian to make this culmination visible to all. The world is grasped *sub specie messias*. The world is experienced by the historian as big with the messiah.[30] This is what the past teaches.

Not only that – it also teaches the means to redemption. The catastrophe of the Roman conquest and the similar situation that confronted Babylonian Jewry with the rise of the Sassanians in the third century C.E. promoted an awareness of the past as a means wherewith to fulfil the divine plan for redemption.

It was through realization of the *Torah*, especially of its social ideals, in the life of Israel, that they [i.e. the rabbis] intended to bring redemption . . . The achievement of justice and mercy, the protection of the rights of the poor and weak, the establishment of a serene and decent social order according to the *Torah's* requirements – these were cruciallly important, because through them, as through prayer, Israel would carry out its side of the messianic contract. Prayer, study, fulfilment of the *Torah*, therefore represented a very vigorous response to the cataclysmic events of the age, and from the rabbis' perspective, embodied more powerful instruments than any other for the achievement of the better age for which Jews longed. Prayer, study, deeds – these three, but of greatest consequence was the legal and judicial enterprise.[31]

The source material for this enterprise was of course the scriptural writings. History was again 'activated' and this time made to yield a fund of praxis. When the rabbis in the academies of Jerusalem and Babylon, in practical terms and as a response to the undiminished demand for redemption, turned to their sources they bent these sources to their own redemptive purposes : that is to say, they used the raw material of scriptural history to construct 'the four cubits of the Law' as a means to living in the Diaspora. Whereas later historians such as Rossi and Gans in the sixteenth century (see Chapter 4 below) took history as matter for contemplation or as source of exhortation, to the sages of the Talmud such an attitude was incomplete to the point of distortion. It was to turn the prescription for the good life into spectacle or narrative.

Negatively, the Talmudic argumentation is illustrated in the sages' explanation for the punishment that God visited on David because of his verse : 'Thy statutes have been my songs in the house of my pilgrimage' (Psalms cxix, 54), i.e. David treated 'statutes' as *belles-lettres*, as 'songs', and this was anathema to the rabbis, for the 'words of *Torah*' were thereby degraded.[32] Positively, in a manner that has been compared to the antithesis propounded by Aristotle between poetry, 'the universal, dealing with such and such a man', and history, 'the particular, dealing with Alcibiades',[33] the Talmud sought to turn the material of the Hebrew scriptures into a system of legal prescriptions, injunctions, etc. If *le'havdil*, Abraham is substituted for Alcibiades one particular is indeed exchanged for another, but the Talmud made this particular of general import by extracting from Abraham's actions, dicta and so on a series of prescriptions, building them into its extended legal corpus. Abraham's purchase of the cave of Machpelah (Genesis xxiii) in which to bury Sarah served, for example, to establish the laws concerning betrothal and also to determine whether the purchase of a field necessarily included all the trees in the field.[34] Similarly, the passage describing those inhabitants of Judah and Jerusalem who failed to respond to Ezra's summons to assemble in Jerusalem (Ezra x, 8) on pain of the forfeiture of their 'substance', was used to define the circumstances in which a court could declare property to be ownerless.[35] It was in this way that history could be fruitfully used as a source and fund of praxis.

The *Halakhah*, in Glatzer's felicitous phrase, looks on itself as 'the germ cell of the messianic kingdom'.[36] If in one sense the *Halakhah* is the epitome of the conservative and the unchanging, it is in another the epitome of revolution in that it looks forward to, and prepares for, the upheaval of the existing order.[37] The *Halakhah* must bear an incommensurable burden because it is charged with the task of redeeming history. It is the instrument whereby Israel fulfils its side of the contract with God in return for which the messianic age will be achieved and the world redeemed. The study of the *Kabbalah*, in the sense of rabbinic tradition, its practice, and thereby the cleaving to God, are the conditions of the messianic future – 'for that is thy life and the length of thy days' (Deuteronomy xxx, 20). The two are interdependent. For this reason a predominant historiographical interest must be the teachers of the Law, of rabbinic tradition, of (in this sense) the *Kabbalah*.

The messianic idea 'powers', as it were, the study of history in such a way as to identify it with the study of *Kabbalah* and to make rabbinic tradition and, in particular, its uninterrupted affiliation with 'the law of Moses from Sinai' its chief subject-matter. In the Jewish context this can only signify the transformation of Jewish history into the bearer of an unchanging body of truth and of Israel into the vehicle through which God has made known to the world His wishes. This does not of course exclude the classification of the historians of the *Kabbalah* in terms of schools, with their particular adventitious motives (e.g. denial of the claims of the Karaites, or the presentation of the ideal Jewish leader).[38] But it does mean that a distinction can be made between what might be termed the enduring values implicitly expressed in the work of a historian and those motives, attitudes, etc. expressed in response to a passing situation. By way of this distinction it can be seen that an enduring preoccupation of the Jewish historian (until the eighteenth century) was his role as expositor of a religious truth.

The term 'expositor' is used advisedly. The Talmud sought to establish for itself a continuity and to see itself as the recipient of a teaching whose ancestry reached back to Moses. He it was who 'received the *Torah* on Sinai and handed it down to Joshua; Joshua to the elders; the elders to the prophets; and the prophets handed it down to the men of the Great Assembly . . . Simon the Just was one of the last survivors of the Great Assembly . . . Antigonos of Socho received the tradition from Simon the Just' etc., down to the days of Hillel and Shammai in the first century C.E.[39] But it is also the case that this teaching, this tradition, was capable of an indefinite extension that formed part of the original revelation. This latter encompassed past, present and future in one. This notion was pointedly emphasised in the argument that 'Scripture, and Mishnah, laws and oral laws not included in the Mishnah, and homiletical tales and the instructions given in the future by a clever student already existed and were given to Moses on Sinai.'[40] But it is also true, as the Talmud explicitly declares, that 'each generation has its interpreters and its scribes'.[41] This certainly permitted a dynamic understanding of the Law, as for example in the 'historicising hermeneutics' that Maimonides devised in order to account for certain of the ceremonial laws.[42] But a dynamic interpretation also contained the danger that generations might fail to comprehend each other. A Midrash for example speaks of a confrontation between Moses and R. Akiba, who will one day unfold the details of the *Halakhah*. Moses fails to understand the new interpretations and 'his strength weakens'. He is not content until he is reassured with a reference to the origin of the new interpretations as '*Halakhah* of Moses at Sinai'.[43]

Therefore, although the *Halakhah* has no history in the sense that it partakes of a continuing and uninterrupted exposition of what was already made manifest at Sinai, it is also true that it might at times be imperfectly understood or the true tradition be perverted. Second, even if the historian can reveal nothing new (was not all revealed to Moses on Sinai?) what he can do – indeed, must do – is to ensure, as the Law is unfolded through the activity of its multitudinous interpreters and teachers, that its decisions and precedents and authorities are protected from misinterpretation, that teacher and pupil are not confused, that decisions have been correctly arrived at, that the true authority has been followed. This tradition must therefore form a main concern of any Jewish historian, for on its correct understanding and transmission depend its present application and future triumph. When the Jewish historian looks back he attempts to trace an unbroken continuity between Moses on Sinai and himself.

By contrast with this enduring tradition the products of Talmudic historiography do not loom large. One of the earliest post-exilic chronicles in Hebrew, dating from the second century C.E., was the *Seder Olam Rabbah* (Greater Order of the World).[44] This is traditionally attributed to R. José b. Halafta. It constitutes a re-telling, with special attention to chronology, of the major events of biblical history from the creation to the time of Daniel and Alexander the Great. Later events down to the Hadrianic period and the Bar Kokhba revolt receive very scanty treatment. A successor to this work was the *Seder Olam Zuta* (Lesser Order of the World, sixth–ninth centuries). The account of the biblical period is much foreshortened and greater emphasis is given to the lineage of the Babylonian exilarchate under the Sassanid dynasty. The author's intention was apparently to prove that the exilarchs, of whom the first was purported to be King Jehoiachin of Judah, exiled by Nebuchadnezzar to Babylon, were of direct Davidic descent but that this was interrupted after the flight of the exilarch Mar Zutra II to the Holy Land in 520.[45]

In socio-political terms it was overwhelmingly the study and practice of the Law, after the destruction of the Jewish state, that served as a bridge to a new world of exile that was both real and fictitious. In the diaspora communities of Babylon, North Africa, France, Germany, Poland–Lithuania, etc. the study of the Law was a practice that arose from the need to preserve Jewish self-government, both for the present and the future. As Zunz put it,

> hopes remained alive and salvation . . . became possible. The former freedom, bound up with legal prescriptions and teachings, remained the ideal in thought and feeling and so the study of the Law became the continuation of political life and practice in the knowledge of justice, so to speak, a pledge of final liberation. Only this study and its representatives could be considered fit and worthy subjects of historical reflection . . .[46]

3 Before the Sixteenth Century

Even if the predominant historiographical modes practised in Israel were the chain of rabbinic tradition and the messianic, it would be absurd and simplistic to assume that these two genres exhausted all historical interest. Such a view would overlook the chronicles of martyrology and persecution that began to appear from the earliest period of the Diaspora.[1] This material does indeed embody a primary response to the major events affecting Jewish life, whether in Babylon, Spain, France or Germany, and constitutes also a reflection on those events.

Thus the famous martyrology of R. Ephraim of Bonn, *Sefer Zekhira* (later 1170s), provoked by the massacres in the Rhineland, England and France during and after the second crusade,[2] is concerned to eulogise and preserve the memory of the martyrs as an inspiration to future generations, to make known the miracles of deliverance, to proclaim the imminence of justice and punishment for the Christians, to describe Jewish attempts at mediation, and to give advice lest a third crusade break out, i.e. that the threatened Jews take refuge in fortified places.[3]

The prevailing tone, however, is practical rather than speculative.[4] An early example of the 'legal' mode was the *Seder Tannaim ve'Amoraim* (Order of the Tannaim and Amoraim) by a Babylonian scholar.[5] It apparently dates from the end of the ninth century, and has two components. The first enumerates the teachers of the Law from Moses to the end of the Saboraic period (sixth to seventh century); the second[6] is a compendium of rules and instructions for deciding between, for example, the decisions of such Talmudic teachers as R. Meir and R. José, R. Jehuda and R. Nehemiah, R. Jehuda and R. Eliezer b. Jacob, and so on. Instructions were also required in the case of decisions whose authors were not given; or where the Talmud had recorded conflicting opinions without giving a decision; or where the same rule had been preserved in different versions.[7]

Another example of historiography conceived in this way was the famous letter of R. Sherira Gaon (986), composed in response to an enquiry from Jacob b. Nissim of Kairuan as to how the Mishnah, Tosephta, Baraitot and Talmud were written, and what was the sequence of the Saboraim and Geonim. R. Sherira's epistle took the form of an ordered exposé of the teachers of the Law, their methods, personal characteristics in teaching and degree of precedence, embracing the period from the Talmud until the tenth century and Sherira's own day.[8] Both the enquiry and the response must be understood, it seems, in the context of an endeavour to authenticate the continuity and accuracy of rabbinic tradition as against the Karaite challenge on both counts.

In the Jewish communities of Germany and Northern France a work in this genre was the *Seder Mekablé Ha'Torah Ve'Lomdeha* (Order of the Recipients of the *Torah* and its Teachers) by R. Jacob b. Samson, one of the pupils of Rashi. This covers the period from the Judges and Prophets to the sages of the Talmud and until the emergence of Mohammed.[9] Another example was the twelfth-century *Seder Tannaim Ve'Amoraim* of R. Judah b. Kalonymos of Speyer. This takes the form of a biographical lexicon to Talmud and Midrash in alphabetical order of sage, together with a note of his sayings, and, on occasion, a commentary thereon by R. Judah.[10] In Spain this historical genre was represented to some small extent by the catalogue of scholars, extending to the author's own day, that Isaac Israeli attached to his work on astronomy, *Yesod Olam* (1310).

In other respects the messianic theme predominated, either in terms of the gradual conquest of the truths of Judaism and the vanquishing of error or in terms of a more or less imminent breakthrough to 'the end of days'. Of the former strain Maimonides was the paramount representative. On the one hand he rejected that kind of history that he 'found amongst the Arabs, books of the generations, the customs of kings, the genealogies of the Arab tribes and books of songs etc., books in which there is no wisdom and no practical benefit but purely a waste of time.' (Commentary to Mishnah Sanhedrin, x, 1)

Maimonides' positive standpoint in respect to history arose from his perception of Judaism as the one true religion, beset in his own day by two counterfeit imitations – Christianity and Islam. Nowhere perhaps is this argued more persuasively than in the Epistle to Yemen of *c*. 1172. But if the truth were to prevail – as prevail it must – then this process could only take the form of victory over the different sources of idolatry and error. Maimonides saw this process at work in the early history of the world, according to the book of Genesis. In the days of Enosh (Genesis v) there had already developed the worship of the stars, sacrificial libations and the cult of wonder-working images. 'And with the passing of time the honoured and revered Name of God was lost from the mouth and mind of man and they did not know Him. The mass of people and women and children knew nothing but the image of wood and stone.' The exceptions were some isolated individuals – Enosh, Methuselah, Noah, etc. Not until Abraham was born and attained to the knowledge of the One God did truth begin to vanquish idolatry and error. At first in Ur and then in Haran and Canaan did Abraham 'proclaim that there was one God for the whole universe and that it was fitting to worship Him.' Abraham brought 'thousands and tens of thousands' to this truth. These are the people referred to as 'the men of the house of Abraham', declared Maimonides. Thenceforward, through Isaac, Jacob and, above all, Moses, the same truth was proclaimed (often in opposition to the relapse into idolatry that characterised the Israelites' exile to Egypt). Now, however, that 'Moses has begun to exercise his prophetic functions, and Israel has been chosen by the Lord as His inheritance, He crowned them with precepts and showed them the way to serve Him and what would be the judgment on idolatry and all who go astray after it.'[11] This process of enlightenment embodied Maimonides' understanding of history.

But more characteristic of Sephardi historiography, as distinct from Ashkenazi, was the messianic strain[12] which often owed much of its force to the clash between Christianity and Islam, either in Spain or the Holy Land.

An important component of this was the continued 'activation' of history in, for example, the field of Biblical commentary. This derived from the traditionally accepted principle – 'the doings of the fathers [patriarchs] are a portent for the children' – and proclaimed a typology of historical structure that made the *Torah* into a repository of future and perhaps even contemporary history, 'because all come into the world in accordance with their deserts'. God brought Greece into the world as a reward for Japhet 'who covered the nakedness of his father'; Rome came into the world as a reward for Esau 'who wept and mourned because Isaac blessed Jacob'; Persia was a reward for Cyrus 'who wept and mourned when the nations destroyed the Temple'.[13] The *Torah* provided the key, or the code, to the understanding of later developments.

This method of exegesis easily lent itself to historico-messianological aims. The *Torah* 'opens the eyes to the future', Nahmanides of Catalonia declared in a sermon, apparently delivered soon after his disputation with Pablo Christiani (Barcelona, 1263). Fortified by this insight, he not only saw the history of the world encapsulated in the seven days of creation,[14] but also, by using to the full the principle that 'the doings of the fathers are a portent for the children' Nahmanides read into the scriptural text a promise of messianic fulfilment. He saw, for example, in the battle successfully waged by the Israelites against the Amalekites a prefiguring of the latter's *final* defeat :

> . . . for a war of this type was the first and last for Israel because Amalek was of the seed of Esau and from him came war upon us with the head of the nations and from the seed of Esau [i.e. Rome] came exile upon us and the last destruction [of the Temple] as our rabbis have said, so that we are today in the exile of Edom but when he is conquered and enfeebled and the many peoples that are with him we shall be saved forever from exile as [the prophet] said, 'and saviours shall come up on Mount Zion to judge the mount of Esau; and the kingdom shall be the Lord's' (Obadiah 1, 21). And now all that Moses and Joshua did to them [i.e. the Amalekites] at the beginning, Elijah and the Messiah son of Joseph will do to their seed . . .[15]

This was the type of thinking that contributed essentially to the formation of a number of historical works that appeared between the twelfth and fifteenth centuries. Their authors (R. Abraham b. Hiyya, R. Abraham Ibn Daud and Don Isaac Abrabanel) were able, by using a variety of techniques – the exegesis of the *Torah* in general and the book of Daniel in particular, astrology, the scrutiny of contemporary events and especially conflicts between Christianity and Islam – to formulate theories of the imminent redemption of Israel, couched in terms of catastrophe rather than evolution. This mode of historiography was eminently programmatic in that it was born of specific circumstances, and has no interest in past or present for their own sake – only in so far as they herald a hoped-for future.

R. Abraham b. Hiyya of Castile (1065–1143) was an astronomer, surveyor, geometer and philosopher. In or shortly before 1129 his *Megilat Ha'Megaleh* (Scroll of the Revealer) appeared, in which he explicitly set out 'to reveal the secret of the redemption'.[16] He was familiar with earlier 'calculations of the end', for example those of Saadya Gaon.[17] He based his own investigations primarily on Genesis, though he took the rest of the *Torah*, including the Book of Daniel, into consideration and also the conjunction of the planets – for Abraham b. Hiyya ascribed to the planetary world an influence over human destiny.[18] So far as Genesis was concerned, since b. Hiyya held to the traditional view that 'the world and its fullness were only created for the sake of the *Torah*',[19] it followed that the whole creation story must refer to the fate of Israel. On this basis he computed that 'the days of the world were 6000 years'.[20] The earliest date when the messianic era could be expected to begin was 4896 A.M. = 1136 C.E. and the latest 5208 A.M. = 1448 C.E.[21]

These calculations belong in part to the apocalyptic atmosphere in Jewish and Christian circles at the time.[22] They are also relevant to the position in which Abraham b. Hiyya found himself between the Christian and Moslem worlds. At the end of the thirty years following the Christian conquest of the Holy Land (Kingdom of Jerusalem, 1099) when the constellation of the stars would return to the sign of the virgin, b. Hiyya foresaw 'war and massacre until the land will almost begin to fall from the hands of Edom . . .' On the consequences and outcome of this war, b. Hiyya refused to speculate because his expressed concern was with the future.[23] But it seems highly probable that his further predictions were bound up with the contemporary politico-military situation – not in Spain, to which b. Hiyya made no reference, but in the Holy Land where the conflict between Christians and Muslims following the first crusade gave hope of redemption. Bar Hiyya was writing at the time when the Seljuk prince Imadeddin Zenki came to power in Mosul in 1127 c.e. and launched the attacks on Syria which later threatened the crusader states and provoked the second crusade. Thus, at the end of the next half-century or so, 4946 a.m. = 1186 c.e. and later, b. Hiyya predicted, using his planet-based calculations, signs of redemption. 'There will be great sorrow in the lands of the Philistines and Edom [Christendom] and Ishmael [Islam] and all the land of Shinaar [Babylon] – during all the days of this conjunction there will not be peace amongst them.' Then, in 4966 a.m. = 1206 c.e., he forsaw 'wars in the land showing signs of the signs of redemption', marked by the beginning of the downfall of the reign of Ishmael. Twenty years later, in 4986 a.m. = 1226 c.e., 'we may be certain that in it [this period] will be revealed signs of our redemption and it will be the head and beginning of our salvation with the help of the Lord.'[24]

Contemporary events, in the messianic perspective, find a more explicit recognition but a less evident embodiment in the *Sefer Ha'Kabbalah* (*c.* 1160) of R. Abraham Ibn Daud of Toledo in Castile.[25] This work can be elucidated at several levels : not only as a contribution to the history of the *Kabbalah* and in the circumstances as an expression of religious polemic directed against the Karaites but also as an exposé of the qualities ideally demanded of Jewish leadership and, furthermore, as a vehicle for the disguised enunciation of a messianic analysis of contemporary events.[26]

Ibn Daud also wrote a history of the emperors of Rome until the beginning of the seventh century, and a history of the kings of Israel in the days of the Second Temple. What was perhaps intended to form a single unit was divided; the author did not wish the demonstration of the continuity of tradition to be interrupted by the inclusion of political events.[27] But all these works support each other and belong together in spirit.

In essence, the *Sefer Ha'Kabbalah* brought together the two dominating themes : the history of the rabbinic tradition and messianic preoccupation. On the one hand, as a legal history, the *Sefer Ha'Kabbalah* began with the Biblical period, and continued with the enumeration of the teachers in the period of the Second Temple and the sequence of Tannaim, Amoraim, Saboraim, Geonim and rabbis in North Africa, Spain and France. This schema was intended to demonstrate, primarily in opposition to the claims of the Karaites, that the evidence of the history of the rabbinic tradition gave unchallengable proof of its unbroken continuity with the scriptural revelation.

The purpose of this book of tradition is to provide students with the evidence that all the teachings of our rabbis of blessed memory, namely, the sages of the Mishna and the Talmud, have been transmitted : each great sage and righteous man having received them from a great sage and righteous man, each head of an academy and his school, having received them from the head of an academy and his school as far back as the men of the Great Assembly, who received them from the prophets, of blessed memory all. Never did the sages of the Talmud, and certainly not the sages of the Mishna, teach anything, however trivial, of their own invention, except for the enactments which were made by universal agreement in order to make a hedge about the *Torah*.'[28]

In actual fact, Ibn Daud's account of the bearers of the oral tradition was all but limited to Spain and did not include the schools of northern France and Germany. (There is however, a mention of flourishing scholars in Narbonne and Rémérupt.)[29] Even so, Ibn Daud's enumeration of the uninterrupted rabbinic chain from Biblical times until his own day served to show that the non-scriptural oral tradition was authentic.

But the Andalus of the eleventh and twelfth centuries was also steeped in the messianic hope, to an extent unequalled, it has been said, since the second century.[30] In the circumstances of the time, when Scripture was seen as a means to the elucidation of the contemporary world, Ibn Daud's *Sefer Ha'Kabbalah* apparently transposed eschatological prophecies of the Book of Daniel into the circumstances of the author's own age and place. In other words, like his Talmudic predecessors, like Abraham b. Hiyya, so too did Abraham Ibn Daud activate the historical promises of the past to give consolatory light to the present. This need arose from the fact that Ibn Daud, born in all probability in Arabic Spain, in Andalus, not later than 1140, had to flee to the Christian north of Castile following the Almohade invasion of Andalus by the forces of Ibn Tumart. Ibn Daud belonged to the many Jews who began a new life in such Moslem–Christian centres as Toledo. Behind them the Jews left the ruins of once flourishing communities: '. . . there were years of war', Ibn Daud wrote in his chronicle, 'of evil decrees and persecutions that fell on the Jews, who were forced to wander from their homes.' He quoted Jeremiah (xv, 2): 'such as are for death, to death; and such as are for the sword, to the sword; and such as are for the famine, to the famine; and such as are for captivity, to captivity.' To this extremity was added Ibn Tumart's attempt to enforce apostasy on the Jews, saying ' "come, and let us cut them off from being a nation, that the name of Israel may be no more remembered." ' Ibn Daud saw the end of Jewish existence 'from the city of Silves at the end of the world until the city of al-Mahdiya'.[31]

In this turmoil he turned to the past and, it seems, deliberately but discreetly interwove, in his history of the rabbinic tradition, an interpretation of the past that referred to the present, in terms of consolation and encouragement. Here Ibn Daud saw the very purpose of history. 'Behold,' he exclaimed, 'how trustworthy are the consolations of our God, blessed be His name, for the chronology of their exile [the Jews'] corresponded to that of their redemption. Twenty-one years passed from the beginning of their exile until the destruction of the Temple and the cessation of the monarchy. Similarly twenty-one years passed from the time its rebuilding was begun until it was completed.'[32] At the end of his history of the *Kabbalah*, Ibn Daud declared his intention of narrating the history of the kings of the Second Temple period, 'in order to refute the Sadducees, who claim that all of the consolatory passages in the books of the prophets were fulfilled for Israel in the days of the Second Temple.'[33] That this was decidedly not the case Ibn Daud sought to show in his exposition of the prophecy of Zechariah (xiv, 1) – 'behold a day of the Lord cometh'. None of the signs foretold by the prophet had yet been witnessed, still less the rule of the house of David – 'the return of which is imminent in our day,' said Ibn Daud.[34]

This confidence came from his messianic-inspired analysis of the circumstances of the mid-twelfth century in conjunction with a schematological analysis of Jewish history. The latter revealed to him that the year 4949 A.M. (= 1188/1189 C.E.), i.e. about twenty-eight years from the time of writing, was to be marked by an event of momentous magnitude. In political terms, Ibn Daud recast the traditional exegesis of Daniel's Four Empires (Babylon,

Persia, Greece and Rome) so as to make allowance for the rise of Islam. This was an accepted modification amongst Spanish–Jewish exegetes and took account of the Christian–Muslim clash in the Holy Land, as expounded, for example, in the work of Abraham b. Hiyya.[35] Ibn Daud however transferred the scene of action from the Holy Land to Spain. It was here that he saw the final struggle approaching. The chronological pattern of empires now became Persia (including Babylon and Media), Greece (including Rome), Persia–Rome, and Islam, the latter branching into oriental Ishmael and the Roman or occidental residue of the third Empire above (Persia–Rome). Furthermore, in Spain Ibn Daud saw a much truer embodiment of the traditional Edom than in Rome and for this reason, for example, spoke of King Alfonso VII of the royal house of Castile in magniloquent terms. Here was the authentic heir to ancient Rome. If it is also recalled that Ibn Daud's reading of history taught him : (*a*) as Rome rose, Israel fell; and (*b*) as Persia favoured Israel, so did it prosper and, conversely, when it persecuted Israel so was it struck by divine retribution – then it is not difficult to construct a vision translatable into contemporary terms and expressive of the salvation of Israel. Given the parlous state of the Jews in Muslim-held Andalus – following the persecutions of the Almoravides and the Almohades who thus rendered themselves subject to divine retribution; given, on the other hand, the renewed impetus of the Reconquista at the hands of the Christian power to the North, was it not possible to see a climactic *dénouement* in the making from which embattled Israel would alone emerge triumphant amidst the downfall of its enemies? That, at any rate, seems to be the conclusion envisaged by Ibn Daud.[36]

Abraham Ibn Daud died about 1180, a martyr 'to the unity of God', according to a report that was not made until some fifty years later. His essay in contemporary history was falsified by events in the all-important particular of Israel. Not only that – from the beginning of the thirteenth century the position of the Jews in Spain markedly and grievously deteriorated so that it came to resemble that of the Jews in northern Europe. Under the influence of religious and national forces Jewish life came under pressure – through public disputations (Barcelona, 1263), measures to suppress the study of the Talmud, physical violence (Toledo, 1212; the 'Shepherds' Crusade', 1320; Navarre, 1328;

Castile, mid-fourteenth century). In 1391 the *juderia* of Seville succumbed to physical attack[37] and large numbers of Jews were forcibly converted to Catholicism, with varying degrees of sincerity, as *conversos*, New Christians or Marranos. Their safety and that of the remaining Jews showed itself exposed to the militancy of the Dominicans and Franciscans as embodied in the anti-Jewish code of Castile (1412), renewed disputations (Tortosa, 1413–14) and in the establishment of the Inquisition in Castile in 1478. But the suppression of Judaising *per se* proved insufficient and in 1492, after the capture of Granada, the last Muslim-held stronghold in Spain, came the decree of banishment. This applied not only to the kingdoms of Castile and Aragon but also to Sardinia and Sicily. In 1497 Portugal also sent its Jewish population into exile. The Jews of the Iberian Peninsula joined those of England and France in a common banishment.

'Each generation has its interpreters and its sages', says the Talmud. The end of the fifteenth century found its interpreter in the person of Don Isaac Abrabanel. Born in Lisbon in 1437, he later became treasurer to King Alfonso V of Portugal. In 1484 he had to flee the country, apparently on account of his supposed involvement with a conspiracy mounted against the crown by the Duke of Braganza and others of the Portuguese nobility. Abrabanel now took service with Ferdinand and Isabella of Castile. He left Spain in 1492, on the signature of the edict of expulsion, and entered the service of the King of Naples. Abrabanel died in Venice in 1508.[38]

Apart from voluminous works of Biblical commentary, Abrabanel also composed three works at the turn of the fifteenth and sixteenth centuries that dealt historically with the advent of the messiah by locating it in a nearby perspective. *Ma'ayenei Ha' Yeshuah* (the Wells of Salvation : Isaiah xɪɪ, 3) took the form of a commentary on the book of Daniel; *Mashmiah Yeshuah* (Announcer of Salvation : Isaiah ʟɪɪ, 7) dealt with all the Biblical passages (save for Daniel) capable of bearing a messianic interpretation; in *Yeshuot Meshiho* (Salvation to His Anointed : Psalm xxvɪɪɪ, 8) Abrabanel considered messianic passages from Talmud and Midrash. As a whole these three works were tantamount to an interpretation of contemporary history in terms of an imminent apocalypse. Abrabanel enunciated a doctrine of the messianic advent that was independent of human volition and effort and akin to a miracle. He identified the year 5263 of the Jewish calendar (= 1503 C.E.) as the beginnings of the messianic age.[39]

In his conviction that an era was coming to an end amidst terror and bloodshed, Abrabanel's teaching has been persuasively compared to the chiliasm of the Taborites and Anabaptists of the fifteenth and sixteenth centuries and the predictions of Savonarola. Likewise, the utterances of Dionysius Ryckel, Johannes Lichtenberger and Antonius Torquatus of Ferrara associated fears of imminent collapse in Imperium and Sacerdotium with Turkish successes – even though the collapse would eventually be overcome.[40]

For all that, Abrabanel's schema and message was rooted in the facts of Jewish history and contemporary experience. With his teaching of the imminent onset of the messianic age he sought to comfort the stricken exiles, demoralised to some extent by losses to Christianity, by voluntary or forcible conversion, and by sustained Christian attacks on Jewish messianism.[41]

> And I said in my heart it is time to work for the Lord to strengthen the weak of hand and the feet of those who stumble, to strive to bring comfort to those who stumble from the exile . . . to seek from the book of the Lord His good tidings when he spoke through His servants the prophets . . . to seek for the end of this world . . . to teach the sons of Judah to uncover their ear . . . for their salvation is near . . .'[42]

What would save Israel, and indirectly all mankind, was the unique relationship of Israel to God. This is not intelligible in historical terms, but its effect in historical terms is not, for that reason, any the less intelligible, for by virtue of this relationship Israel enjoys a history *sui generis*. The normal laws of historical causality do not apply here in that the divine government of the world is in the case of Israel direct and individual and not mediated through any other influences (e.g. planetary) – 'The people of Israel is unique in its divine leadership . . .'[43] This is the force that gives Israel its assurance of eternity. Abrabanel here refers to Malachi (III, 6): 'for I the Lord change not; and Ye, O sons of Jacob [Israel] are not consumed.'[44] Moreover, Abrabanel's knowledge of the history of the ancient world showed him that whereas Greece, pagan Rome, Assyria, Persia and Babylon had all succumbed to history, Israel alone had survived and defied the forces of disintegration.[45]

But this assurance is in itself no safeguard against decline and fall.[46] It certainly did not safeguard Israel against the dispersion and exile that were the punishment for its disobedience to the divine Law. This was the most anguished of all the questions to which Abrabanel and his generation had to address themselves. His response was couched in the form of a messianic theory which may be said to have its *point de départ* in this very exile. But it was also indebted to the political and historical circumstances of Abrabanel's own day. Abrabanel treated historical data as a 'mere material for the apocalypticist'.[47]

He had first to refute the Christian claim that the messiah had come in the person of Jesus; second, that the restoration of the Temple after the return of the exiles from Babylon already represented a partial fulfilment of Israel's own promise of redemption. On both counts he resorted to a mixture of religio-scriptural and historical argument; as to the Christian claim, not only, for example, that Isaiah's references to 'the redemption' had a physical and political connotation that could in no way be reconciled with 'the spiritual redemption as is the way of the peoples or the period of the Second Temple'[48] but also that Christendom could not be identified with that 'Fifth Kingdom' of Daniel (II, 44) which would 'consume' the previous four and 'stand forever'. Abrabanel argued that whereas

all Africa and most of Asia took the religion of Jesus Christ when they accepted it in Rome, after some years they left it and took the religion of Mohammed who are most of the world and there only remained in that religion [Christianity] but the relatively few people of Europe . . . and even today most of the world believes not in Jesus . . . and this contradicts what is written . . .'[49]

As to the Jewish arguments concerning the messianic connotation of the period of the Second Commonwealth, here Abrabanel enumerated ten conditions, drawn from the prophetic writings, the non-fulfilment of which made it impossible to consider the Second Temple even a partial fulfilment of the divine promise: the appearance of a king–messiah from the seed of David to rule Israel; the gathering of the exiles; retribution for the enemies of

Israel; the prosperity of the land of Israel; the wisdom of Israel and sanctity of its land; the return of prophecy; the renewal of divine signs and miracles; the end of the exile; the acceptance by all peoples of faith in the One God; and the resurrection of the dead.[50]

The elimination of these two positions now made it possible for Abrabanel to show precisely why the present age – the sixth millenium by Jewish reckoning and the fifteenth to sixteenth century by Christian – must be considered 'the end of days'. He had no doubt that he could see all the traditional symptoms, proclaimed in the Talmud, of the 'birth-pangs of the messiah' : the spread of heresy, the dissolution of family ties, the complete and utter collapse of Jewish collective life in the land of Israel and the Diaspora, physical suffering, famine, scorn for learning and scholars.[51] All this signalled the final degeneration of the perfection of the first man, a process ultimately attributable to his primal fall.

This was a doctrine of collapse and catastrophe to which only a miraculous deliverance could correspond. The prototype for this deliverance was the Exodus from Egypt with its accompaniment of divine power (though with the difference that the coming redemption would directly affect all mankind); and, similarly, the messiah would be akin to Moses.

The imminent messianic age was in this sense unpolitical.[52] But in the sense that the doctrine took account of contemporary politics in which it saw the agencies of a cosmic drama of incommensurable magnitude, it was anything but unpolitical. The exegesis of Daniel and Abrabanel's interpretation of contemporary European diplomacy came together to form a heady mixture.

Methodologically speaking, Abrabanel activated history, in the fashion of the Talmud, by transposing certain prophetic utterances to a later epoch. When Daniel (xi, 18) declared that 'after this shall he set his face unto the isles and take many; but a captain shall cause the reproach offered by him to cease; yea, he shall cause his own reproach to return upon him' Abrabanel (following Abraham b. Hiyya) understood 'captain' to refer to the emperor Constantine

who went to Constantinople and captured all the isles of the archipelago and all the rest of the land of Egypt and Greece

B*

and the beauteous land and built Constantinople and called it after his own name, about which it is said 'but a captain shall cause reproach offered by him to cease', i.e. that the captain Constantine caused Rome to cease which was his reproach and head of his faith and made in its stead a second reproach and from then onwards there were two heads in Edom, Rome and Constantinople.'[53]

Crucial to Abrabanel's messianology was the identification of the Fourth and Fifth Kingdoms referred to by Daniel. In the Jewish perspective the latter could only be that of Israel, in fulfilment of the divine assurance. But Abrabanel again activated history and drew on the utterances of Isaiah, Jeremiah and Obadiah so as to identify a continuity between the traditional understanding of the Fourth Kingdom as pagan Rome (common to both Jews and Christians) and contemporary Rome.[54] The Fourth Kingdom still held sway. But what of Islam? How could this inescapable factor, for which Daniel apparently made no provision, be included in the schema? Abrabanel overcame this problem by, as it were, making Islam part of a movement of continual dissent within Christendom.

It was in this way that he was able to bring together his Biblical exegesis and the facts of contemporary history. Abrabanel saw the world divided (save for Israel) into the warring camps of Edom and Ishmael. The first he carefully distinguished from the inhabitants of Edom in the vicinity of Jerusalem; rather, he explained, he used the term to designate 'the Christians and all the inhabitants of the land of Italy.' In this sense the Edomites were the heirs to Greece and Rome.[55] The Ishmaelites on the other hand comprised Islam, in whom Abrabanel saw the contemporary Turks as the heirs to Babylon and Persia.[56] These were the protagonists in a catastrophic and climactic east–west conflict between the two sworn enemies of Israel from which the latter would emerge *tertium gaudens*; and this was foreshadowed in Ezekiel's vision of Gog coming against the land of Israel. If the prophet foresaw (xxxviii, 21) that 'every man's sword shall be against his brother', then Abrabanel commented, 'and these brothers are Edom and Ishmael'.[57]

Abrabanel knew the messianico-historical work of Abraham b. Hiyya[58] and restored his notion of a final conflict in and around the Holy Land, as against the Hispanic orientation of R. Abraham Ibn Daud. The conflict would have two centres, Abrabanel expected, the first in the eastern Mediterranean where Muslim Egypt would succumb to an attack from the Christian powers and suffer the punishment predicted by Isaiah at the hands of Edom.[59] Then the campaign would move to the vicinity of Jerusalem for an engagement between Edom and Ishmael in which the lost Ten Tribes of Israel would participate, for it was not fitting that the redemption of the Jews should take place without Jewish contribution – even though this could have no effect on a campaign which lay in God's hands. What Abrabanel foresaw in fact was a divinely inspired conjunction of forces whereby the two adversaries of Israel would destroy each other.[60] After the first engagement in the Holy Land in which the Christians were defeated, though not conclusively so, Islam would press home its advantage through successful assaults on the Christian fleets in the eastern Mediterranean, capture Rhodes and Venice, and invade Italy. Here in Rome all the destruction awaiting Edom, according to the prophecies of Isaiah, Jeremiah and Obadiah, was to be accomplished. But this would not leave Islam victorious. As Rome drew its last breath the messiah would reveal himself. Now unrolls the whole panorama of the physical and spiritual redemption of Israel, including the resurrection of the generations of the Exile.[61]

'Constantinople was defeated by the Persians, who are today called Turks and afterwards the exile is completed.'[62] These words elucidate the bond between Abrabanel's eschatological vision of redemption and contemporary historical reality. Following the Turkish capture of Constantinople (the capital of eastern Christendom) in 1453, Abrabanel saw the success of Turkish power against the Tartar Khan of the Crimea and in the Black Sea area, he saw Turkey under Sultan Mehmed II gain control of the Eastern Mediterranean and force Venice to make peace. He saw Turkish conquests in Bosnia, Herzegovina and Wallachia. When Mehmed died in 1481 his sole setbacks were the failure to take Belgrade or Rhodes. But under his successor Bayezid II (1481– 1512) Turkish attacks in south-eastern Europe took them as far as Kanczug, and in the campaign against Venice they won the strongpoints of the island of Cephalonia and, in 1497, Lepanto on the Gulf of Corinth. All this made it possible for the Turks to attack the Venetian mainland. Moreover, the Christian powers showed their divisions, and nowhere more dramatically so than in Charles VII's invasion of Italy in 1494 with the largest army Europe had yet seen, in his entry into Rome and his conquest of Naples. All this was grist to Abrabanel's messianic mill for it was precisely at this time of the apparent dissolution of Christendom, confronted by triumphant Islam, that he was meditating and composing his messianic trilogy. Moreover, the powers in east and west were warring precisely at a time when Israel's own fortunes were at their nadir. It was eschatology become history – that historiographical genre in which the messianic component blends indistinguishably with the historical, in which – as in the case of R. Abraham Ibn Daud or R. Abraham b. Hiyya – the historical world is seen *sub specie messias.*

4 The Beginning of Modernity

The work of Abrabanel can be regarded as the swan-song of classical historico-messianology. This remains so, despite the temptation that the sack of Rome (1527), the Reformation and Counter-Reformation, and the wars of religion might be expected to offer to eager 'calculators of the end'. There were indeed those, such as R. Abraham b. R. Eliezer Halevi (born Spain 1460, died Jerusalem 1528), who saw in Luther a disguised Jew. R. Abraham brought the fall of Constantinople, the exile of the Jews and the advent of the messiah into one schema of salvation: 'from the time that Constantinople was conquered by the great Turkish king, from then began the time of the end . . .'[1] Certain Lutheran teachings must without fail arouse a congenial response amongst many Jews. At the end of the sixteenth century, for example, the chronicler-historian, David Gans, wrote of Luther with evident sympathy. He described him as

> a great scholar in their writings [who] examined, studied and composed many works and walked in the footsteps of Johannes Hus . . . and made the religion of the Pope odious and divided the heart of the Christians and wanted to burn and destroy all images, and they should no longer pray to Mary, mother of their anointed, and not to his twelve apostles and that bishops and clergy should take wives . . .'[2]

Messianic speculation turned rather to the mystical level and away from the historical. But it did not for that reason abandon the latter. It seems that Isaac Luria, of the new mystical school at Safed, had some expectation of 1575 as the year of redemption.[3] In Prague R. Judah Löw b. Bezalel (= the Maharal), later in the sixteenth century, brought his theory of redemption into the closest possible contact with the position of Israel among the nations. 'The content of the messiah is the content of the present world.'[4] On the other tack, the Maharal was perhaps the first to argue that in a world community of nations or peoples, it could not but be anomalous that one people – Israel – should find itself dispersed and in subjection : 'exile is in itself a proof and clear evidence of redemption and this because there is no doubt that exile is a distortion and departure from order in that the Holy One Blessed Be He put each people in the place appropriate to it and ordered Israel in the place appropriate to them, i.e. the Land of Israel, and exile from their place is an utter distortion and departure.'[5] This followed from the Maharal's very clear perception of a plurality of peoples, the Biblical division of humanity into nations, as exemplified in the episode of the Tower of Babel. The Maharal placed this concept at the very centre of his historical analysis. Here was a division that belonged to the very order of the world.[6] Each nation was a composite of matter and form which through it expressed its individuality.[7]

This made each nation unique. It was not a mere geographic or historical entity but also spiritually distinct from its neighbour. Many factors gave to each people its distinctive characteristics : its script and language – 'for a script relates to each people in that each people has a special script and not all peoples use the same script';[8] its own form of government;[9] its own religion and religious aspirations;[10] its own legal order (*Seder*).[11] But the perception of the uniqueness of Israel did not turn the Maharal into a historian.

Rather, at the specific historical level the messianic urge made itself felt in the careers of such men as Asher Lemmlein, David Reuveni and Solomon Molko; most notably, of course, in the movement inspired by Sabbetai Zevi a century later.[12]

But the study of history in the sixteenth century took a different path. For reasons that are by no means clear but undoubtedly relate to the growing interest taken by the Renaissance and the Protestant Reformation in the culture of Israel, Jewish historians began to take a dispassionate interest in the non-Jewish world. R. Joseph Ha'Cohen's *History of the Kings of France and Turkey* (1554) and R. Elijah Kapsali's slightly earlier histories of Turkey and Venice suggest this conclusion. Even more noteworthy were the consequences for those scholars who occupied themselves with Jewish history.

Generally in the Christian world in the sixteenth and seventeenth centuries – in the period between Melancthon and Leibniz, say – the historico-theological understanding of universal history began to dissolve and give way to a historico-philosophical understanding.[13] Jean Bodin, for example, was the first historian and thinker to challenge the eschatological concept of Daniel's Four Kingdoms.[14] Bodin's Jewish contemporaries were exposed to these Christian influences, but their reaction was *sui generis*. When modernity entered, it did so through the introduction of some account of the non-Jewish world and the attempt to integrate the latter with events in Jewish history. But this must necessarily require some weakening of the idea of the Four Kingdoms. In other words, the Hebrew Bible is no longer altogether adequate on its own as a medium for the ordering and comprehension of the historical world. The new history therefore also required the use of non-Jewish sources – albeit *à contre-coeur*, in some cases – and the presentation of the lessons to be derived from historical study in terms hitherto more familiar to the Christian than the Jewish world. The Jewish historians of this period were not writing for scholars, and this may help to account for the novel argument that an improved knowledge of the past would equip Jews to discuss matters of mutual interest with Christians, that a knowledge of the Christian world was, as such, a necessity for the Jew who lived in a Christian environment.[15] Many historians (for example R. Abraham Zacuto, Gedaliah Ibn Yahya, R. Solomon Ibn Verga) were exiles from Spain, or the descendants of exiles, and their works are also in part an attempt to seek an explanation for their hard fate.[16]

The basic theme underwent no change : this still remained the history of the rabbinic tradition. But the unfolding has lost its practical urgency, and is intermingled with other themes.

The new modernity also made itself evident in the treatment of persecution. In his *Shevet Yehuda*, Tribe, or Staff, of Judah, first published in Turkey in *c.* 1554 (the title may be a pun on the Spanish meaning of *Verga* = rod), R. Solomon Ibn Verga (second half of the fifteenth century to the first quarter of the sixteenth century) sought to explain objectively and naturalistically the hostility to which the Jews were exposed throughout their history. Ibn Verga was himself a refugee from Spain who then lived for some years in Portugal where he was forcibly converted to Christianity. But in 1506 he was able to leave Portugal and settle in Italy, where he apparently became familiar with the ideas of men such as Guicciardini and Machiavelli.[17]

It seems that the earliest version of *Shevet Yehuda* may go back to the fifteenth century.[18] But it was in about 1520, in Italy, that it took its present form at the hands of Ibn Verga. It became an account of anti-Jewish persecutions from the time of the destruction of the Second Temple until the author's own day. Ibn Verga used earlier chronicles and martyrologies which he interspersed with imaginary dialogues supposedly held at a Christian court and amongst Christians. The interlocutors are a wise king Alfonso of Spain and his intimate counsellor Thomas. They serve as mouthpieces for Ibn Verga's own views. Two features characterise their dialogue : first, the notion of religious relativity. This is a notable distinction from R. Ephraim of Bonn, for example, who had seen in Christianity a form of idolatry. But in the *Shevet Yehuda*, King Alfonso argues that

> it is agreed by all that the religions only exist by virtue of the imagination. The Jew will think by virtue of his representation that there is no other religion and no other faith except his faith and he who believes in anything else is in his eyes an animal. The Christian imagines that the Jew is only an animal in human form . . . And if you ask a Moslem then he will say that hell is full of both of us . . .

Similarly with the Sabbath : Alfonso asks, why did Moses, Jesus and Mohammed choose different days to celebrate the Sabbath? Thomas replies : 'Moses thought that it was fitting to honour the day of rest for on it God rested . . . The prophet of the Ishmaelites said that man rejoices on the day that he finishes his labour and therefore ordained Friday, on which day the work of creation was concluded. And Jesus chose Sunday for it is fitting to give honour to the beginning of creation . . .'[19]

The other distinctive feature of *Shevet Yehuda* is the quest for a natural explanation of Israel's lowly state. Here Ibn Verga also speaks in his own person, taking up a theme first raised by Alfonso. What is important in this presentation is Ibn Verga's attempt to comprehend Jewish suffering in general, and in Spain in particular, not solely in terms of divine punishment but also in naturalistic terms, inspired by the interaction of political forces and the conduct of the Jews themselves. Again, there is an instructive comparison with R. Ephraim of Bonn who had seen the crusaders as in some way a reincarnation of Pharaoh and Haman (though this had also not prevented him from understanding the motives of the crusaders).

As to the first, Ibn Verga declared that 'generally the Kings of Spain and France, the nobility, the learned and all the men of dignity were friendly to the Jews and hatred only existed in the people who envied the Jews.'[20]

But what sins have the Jews committed to justify their sufferings, asks the king. Thomas replies :

> I have never seen a man of reason hate the Jews and there is none who hates them except the generality of the people, and for this there is a reason, for the Jew is arrogant and always seeks to rule and it would never be thought that they are exiles and slaves driven from people to people, but rather that they seek to show themselves lords and masters, therefore the masses envy them.

When the Jews were poor, did it then ever happen that they were accused of using blood, Thomas asked.[21] Speaking in his own name, Ibn Verga gave a religious dimension to Jew-hatred in seeking to understand his self-posed question, why the Jews should be singled out for a degree of suffering far in excess of anything meted out to peoples far more sinful than were the Jews. He first answered by quoting Amos iii, 2 : 'You only have I known of all the families of the earth, therefore I will visit upon you all your iniquities.' He then added that the sons were suffering for the sins of their fathers; that 'if the merit of the Jews was not great, then the Exile persists for natural reasons, because of religious hatred and the desire of the ruler to subject everyone to his faith and belief'; all the more so, 'because our religion forbids eating and drinking with them . . .' He next spoke of the crucifixion, of envy arising from three sources – religion, women, money; of the fact that 'the people grew accustomed to swearing falsely' and, lastly, of the arrogance of the Jews.[22]

Something of the same realism is also present in the rabbinical histories of the sixteenth century. This was continued in the work of men such as Abraham Zacuto, Gedaliah Ibn Yahya and R. David Gans. The first two hailed from Spain and Gans from

Germany. All were touched in varying degrees by an unwillingness to accept tradition without scrutiny and by the need to include matter relating to the non-Jewish world. But they had no great historical self-esteem or vocational regard. They did not consider their historical works to be products of true scholarship. They clearly considered their histories to belong to a lesser order of scholarship than the actual instruction in the Law. Of course, it still remained of supreme importance to trace the correct authority and true tradition, but such matters as legal method and the rules for arriving at a decision are all but ignored. In fact this branch of historical study became in the sixteenth century increasingly academic and theoretical. It lost its actuality and urgency in the realm of *praxis*. Gans for example, explicitly declared that matters of 'impurity and purity, of prohibition and permission did not arise' from his book. It was only by reason of this limitation, he writes, that he undertook the history at all.[23] Zacuto, the astronomer who had prepared the navigational tables for Columbus in 1492, explained in the preface to his *Sefer Yuhasin* (Book of Genealogies)[24] that although his intention was to recapitulate the sages of the Talmud and their decisions, 'I will not boast that this is a deep science'.[25]

On the other hand, Zacuto did take issue with Maimonides and argue that despite the latter's anti-historical stance in his commentary to the *Mishnah*,[26] there 'was great benefit' in specifying the interrelationship of the rabbis quoted, 'in strengthening our hands in the Oral Law, in following the tradition up to Moses the master of the prophets who received it from the Holy One Blessed Be He and how it came from sage and righteous man to sage and righteous man to the light of the world . . . ask thy father, and he will declare unto thee, thine elders and they will tell thee' (Deuteronomy xxxii, 7).[27] Zacuto then quoted sundry earlier rabbinical authorities who had emphasised the need, indeed the merit and obligation, to quote a dictum in the name of he who had first uttered it (*Pirkei Avoth*, vi, 6). Zacuto also argued that a correct chronology was an indispensable means to determining what the actual decision was, for 'the law follows the last from Abbaye onwards . . .' He quoted in his support R. Samson b. Isaac of Chinon (author of *Sefer Kerituth*) to the effect that the Law could not be known unless it was also known who its teachers were and when they had lived.[28]

The first five sections of the *Sefer Yuhasin* follow the chain of rabbinic tradition partly in chronological and partly in alphabetical sequence, from the Creation to the author's own day, virtually. It includes also tables of the Tannaim, the Amoraim and the Geonim in alphabetical and chronological order. For the later generations of scholars Zacuto confessed to his reliance on R. Abraham Ibn Daud.[29] For Rashi and subsequent commentators in Ashkenaz and Spain, Zacuto gave their works, genealogies and some particulars of their lives.[30]

It is already noteworthy that at an earlier point in describing the years after the destruction of the Second Temple, Zacuto adds, 'and thus it is in the histories of the Christians'.[31] But this is no real preparation for the sixth and last section of his work which is largely devoted to an attempt to integrate the Jewish and the Gentile past. Zacuto evidently approached this part of his work with a certain amount of diffidence. This did not arise from any doubt concerning its utility but rather from the nature of the sources. In his introductory note to Part VI he argued that the knowledge of what has happened to every people, and in particular what has happened to the people of Israel, will strengthen faith in the power of God; such knowledge, furthermore,

> will be very useful to Jews who live amongst Christians to dispute with them about their religion and I have therefore mentioned some men outside our faith whom it would not be fitting to mention . . . in the same way as the holy *Torah* similarly refers to evil men . . . and you should not therefore think that all that is written in their chronicles whose words I have quoted is all truth like the words of our holy *Torah* . . .[32]

The first five periods in the history of the world are established by reference to the history of Israel (from the Creation to the Babylonian exile) but they also include references to the emergence of music in Crete, to the birth of Persephone and Prometheus, to the reign of Dido in Tyre overlapping with that of David, to Greek philosophers (Isocrates, Plato, Epicurus) and sundry Persian rulers. From the sixth age onwards ('beginning of the realm of England', at the end of the fifth millenium A.M.) Zacuto's work is even more disparate with scattered, uncoordinated references to Ptolemy, Jesus, John the Baptist, Philo and Livy, the

Emperor Constantine, the sack of Rome by the Goths, the coronation of Charlemagne, the work of Ibn Roshd and so on.[33]

A history of the *Kabbalah* combined with a presentation of the non-Jewish world also characterised Gedaliah Ibn Yahya's *Shalshelet Ha'Kabbalah* (Chain of Tradition, first published in Venice, 1587). Ibn Yahya was born in 1515 in Italy where he spent most of his life. In the 1570s he lived for some years in Ferrara and in 1575 he emigrated to Egypt and died in Alexandria in 1578. The *Shalshelet Ha'Kabbalah* was written, according to the author, in response to a complaint from his son that, after the work of R. Abraham Ibn Daud and Maimonides' introduction to his *Mishneh Torah*, nothing existed that traced the further transmission of rabbinic doctrine. In filling this gap – a period of some three and a half centuries – such benefits were seen as instruction in the Law, an incentive to study on the model of earlier generations, the illustration of continuity, the inspiration to martyrdom and the additional reinforcement that knowledge would bring to the defence against hostile critics, to say nothing of an increased awareness of the workings of providence.[34]

Ibn Yahya was confessedly ignorant of much of the necessary subject-matter and therefore relied not only on the classical sources but also on his predecessors – R. Sherira Gaon, R. Abraham Ibn Daud, Maimonides, Abraham Zacuto as well as 'the most reliable chroniclers' of the Christian world.[35] The first part of the book follows the rabbinic tradition from the creation to the European teachers of the sixteenth century, by way of Moses, Joshua and the sages and rabbis who compiled the Mishnah, to R. Ashi (d. 427) and Ravina (d. *c.* 500) who, traditionally, compiled the Gemara. The second part testifies to Ibn Yahya's wide interests in coins, measurements, the planets, medicine, the soul, witchcraft, etc. The third part is 'a chain of the sages of the peoples and the decrees against Israel and the new things that emerged in each generation.' This last section partakes of the nature of a chronicle and ranges from the Garden of Eden to the sixteenth century and includes much legendary and mythological material.[36]

The work of R. David Gans brought together these new approaches to such effect and in such a manner that though his work is essentially a chronicle, he has been described as 'the first Jew in Ashkenaz to concern himself with professional history'.[37]

This is a reference to Gans' *Zemach David* (The Offspring of David, first published in Prague, 1592). Gans was born in Lippstadt (Westphalia) in 1541. He studied in his youth at the *Yeshiva* at Frankfurt a.M. and then at the even more celebrated *Yeshiva* in Cracow directed by R. Moses Isserlis. He moved to Prague in 1564 where as a pupil of R. Judah Löw b. Bezalel (the Maharal of Prague) he participated to the full in the intellectual ferment, encouraged by the Hapsburg ruler Rudolf II, that characterised sixteenth-century Prague, Jewish and Christian.

This was facilitated by the contacts that Prague enjoyed with the Jewish centres of Cracow and Venice; and by the relative harmony between Jew and Christian. In a sermon delivered at Poznan in 1592 the Maharal of Prague warmed to the fact that in his day expulsions marked Jewish suffering, rather than the massacres and crushing financial extortions of former times. In commenting on *Pirkei Avoth* the Maharal said : 'While the ancients fulfilled the *Torah* under dire poverty and under the persecution of the Gentiles, now we sit in our homes, each one relaxed.'[38]

In this relatively tranquil time and place, Gans eagerly espoused the work of the Renaissance – the spread of printing, for example, and the discoveries that made known matters 'hidden and concealed from [our] predecessors'. He was himself eminent as astronomer, mathematician and cosmographer. 'Blessed be the Lord who multiplied His loving-kindness over us and showed us marvels.'[39] Gans enjoyed friendly relations with Johannes Müller, Kepler and Tycho Brahe, for whom he translated certain astronomical tables from Hebrew into German. He died in 1613.

Gans had an omnivorous intellectual curiosity and it was clearly in order to quench this curiosity that he turned to the study of history and in 1592 published his chronicle, *Zemach David*. He also hoped to preserve for posterity the memory of the great scholars of the past and present, 'for without the pen of the scribe there is no memorial of the first men and the last.' He took pride in the fact that he was the only such memorialist to recount the past from the creation of the world to his own time, 'in sequence, as I have done in this book'. Gans in fact essayed more than a mere historico-literary feat. Rather, he sought to create a Jewish historical consciousness in the sense of responsiveness to contemporary Christian reality.[40] He would blend the hitherto exclusive rule of the Biblical past with the world of the sixteenth century. If, hitherto, the Jew had looked on the period of exile – the Diaspora – as an undifferentiated stretch of time[41] now, Gans argued, such a Jew must acknowledge the existence of a changing reality.

Gans combined this radically new approach to the contemporary world with considerable derogation from the role of the *Halakhah*. Although his use of personal reminiscence contributes to the knowledge of the rabbinical schools and the cultural history of central Europe, the book is further testimony to the degeneration of the study of the Law and its transference from the realm of injunction and *praxis* to that of academic study. Gans' work was *not* concerned with decision-making but was of altogether a lesser order of importance; it was history and not, therefore, a prescription for action. For this reason, when Gans does come to talk of the lessons of history, these are formulated, not in terms of legal prescriptions but in terms of exhortation and moralising sentiment.[42]

Gans took as his sources the Hebrew Scriptures, the Apocalyptic, aggadic and Midrashic writings, the more important legal commentators and expositors, philosophers, earlier Jewish chroniclers, the reports of eye-witnesses and his own personal experiences. In the introduction to Part I of *Zemach David*, that dealing with Jewish history, he explained that he had 'knocked on the doors of the sages' and made a summary of the works of his predecessors, such as R. Sherira Gaon, Ibn Daud, Maimonides, Zacuto, etc.,

> because most of the men of our generation wish to learn all the *Torah* while standing on one foot. Therefore and so that they should not trouble themselves and become impatient and spend their time in researching and exploring the works of the ancients, I decided to meet their wish with this short book . . . [which] is only a calendar and reference to the books of the ancients and there will not be clarified in it but the general principles of the times.[43]

'Even sucklings at school can copy and compose a book such this', he adds. He was not writing for scholars, 'only for . . . householders like myself'.[44]

The customary re-telling of the Scriptural narrative follows the introductory remarks. Gans gave special attention to the kings of the period of the Second Temple and of the house of Herod,

taking care all through his compilation to date events and person-
alities according to the traditional calendar. Gans' later pages (in
Part I) recount the generations of Amoraim, and the scholars of
the Saboraic and Geonic periods. In modern times he chronicles
in a typical passage the lives of, say,

> Rabbenu Gershom, The Light of the Exile, of France, the
> author of decrees, and R. Jacob b. Yakar, and the sage and
> poet R. Solomon Ibn Gabirol, and they were the teachers of
> Rashi and all died in the year 4830 and in their days lived
> R. Moses Ha'Darshan of Narbonne and R. Judah b. Barzilai
> who wrote the *Sefer Ha'Ittim* and R. Joseph Tov Elem who
> is quoted by all the codifiers and R. Zerachia author of *Ha'-
> Meor* and other great men singled out by name in [Zacuto's]
> *Sefer Yuhasin.*[45]

Gan's use of personal reminiscence is illustrated in his concluding eulogy of the benefactor of Prague Jewry, Mordecai Meisl,
and, even more so, in his short mention of the encounter between
the Maharal of Prague, and the Emperor Rudolf II on the first
day of the week, Adar 3, 5352 (= Sunday 16 February 1592).
'The great and meritorious luminary, our master the Emperor
Rudolf' summoned the Maharal 'and gave him a warm and
gracious welcome and spoke with him face to face as a man speaks
with his neighbour but the substance and manner of their words
are closed, sealed and hidden.'[46]

In the second part of *Zemach David*, that dealing with Gentile
history, Gans explained that he would 'reproduce from the
chroniclers, i.e. from the books of the memorials of all the times
of the four empires – Babylon, Persia, Greece, Edom [Rome] and
all the rulers that reigned over them from the time of Nimrod
the son of Cush, the first king of Babylon, to the time of our ruler
the Emperor Rudolf II and the many deeds that were performed
in their days.' The separation between Parts I and II served 'to keep
the holy and the profane apart'.[47]

Gans necessarily used non-Jewish sources, some of which he
enumerated – for example Cyriacus Spangenburg, Hubertus Gel-
cius, Laurence Faust, Georg Cassius, Martin Barik.[48] His prefatory
remarks illuminate his reservations in coupling secular history
with that of rabbinical tradition, notwithstanding the division he
had operated :

I see from the outset that many will gape at me and will accuse me of perversity and will think ill of me because I have written from books not written by the children of Israel, in addition to which the second part of this book is as the stories of wars and other things. In their eyes is this not secular writings and . . . in their opinion will it not in any case be forbidden to read them on the Sabbath? I will certainly not argue or spend time over my apology for many of the great ones of Israel will be my defence and shield.

Gans cited the precedent of those (Jewish) philosophers who quoted Aristotle and of historians such as Abraham Zacuto, Joseph Ha'Cohen and Abraham Farissol who 'ate the kernel and threw away the shells'. He also cited in self-defence the ruling by his earlier teacher, R. Moses Isserlis, in favour of the permissibility of reading secular matter on the Sabbath, providing it were couched in Hebrew, as against the ruling of R. Joseph Caro who prohibited such reading both on Sabbath and weekday.[49]

Gans also referred to the Book of Esther, asking if this work did not form part of the history of the Medes and Persians; to Jeremiah (xviii, 13): 'Ask ye now among the nations, who hath heard such things'; and to Deuteronomy (iv, 32): 'For ask now of the days past, which were before thee, since the day that God created man upon the earth . . .'[50] But in following this implied authorisation to use Gentile sources, Gans acknowledged that they were not composed 'in a spirit of holiness' and it could not therefore be said that the events they narrated 'were certainly in this or that way for even an event which took place today in our very presence eye-witnesses will see in different aspects. There are enemies and detractors as there are lovers and laudators.' And how much greater must the possibilities of error be when these reports had to pass from language to language![51]

Gans followed initially but with some uncertainty the pattern of the history of the Four Empires in the traditional exegesis of Daniel – Babylon, Persia, Greece and Rome. This, he pointed out, was the pattern of the history of the Gentile world as understood by the sages of old, 'until the coming of our Messiah', and this pattern had also been followed by 'the sages of the peoples', though the latter spoke of the 'Four Monarchies'.[52] But he also acknowledged that even during the period of the Four Empires, 'there were great and powerful rulers'.[53] In any case, although he had to extend his framework with the rise of Mohammed, he concentrated on the history of Europe.

This was couched to some extent in terms of the spread of Christianity but very largely in terms of dynasties and monarchs, their reigns, their conquests and defeats. Of Attila, for example, Gans writes :

> He was the King of the Huns who are in Hungary, a man of blood whom they called the rod of wrath of the Holy One Blessed Be He who kept his land with five hundred thousand men and captured and destroyed many cities and states in the lands of the east. After that he turned to Germany and went through Austria and Bavaria and captured Augsburg and invaded Switzerland and captured and destroyed many towns and descended to the Rhine where he took Strasbourg, Speyer, Worms, Mainz and Cologne and many towns besides and every place he came to he burnt . . .[54]

Social factors are more prominent in later centuries as, for example, the Peasants' Revolt of 1525. Gans described this as the result of the refusal of the peasants to be ruled by any lord or master.

> It began in Württemberg and Swabia and extended to the Rhineland in Alsace also to the bishopric of Salzburg and to Franconia and Thuringia and there gathered from all these regions an uncountable number of people and at first they asked for twelve articles, all good and worthy, but when their strength increased they threw off the yoke of servitude from their neck and the peasants from Franconia rose up and destroyed all the houses of the priests and burnt twenty-three of them. And all the governors and the rulers were chased from the land . . . and all who refused to give them signatures and documents and to give them help with men and money the peasants attacked and ravaged their armies and set their towns on fire. Then all the princes of Germany assembled their forces and attacked the peasants . . .[55]

Amongst the advantages to be derived from the study of Gentile history such as this Gans counted its demonstration of the workings of providence in protecting Israel, amidst wars in which, 'merely on account of changes in custom' between 'the Papal party and the Lutheran party', more than a million Christians had been killed. Gans quoted Exodus xi, 7 : 'against any of the children of Israel shall not a dog whet his tongue'; history also taught a man in high position to be humble, to be wary of lesser enemies as well as greater, not to quarrel with those who are more powerful; it showed that providence punished the wicked in this world; that moral teachings said to proceed from the mouth of an emperor are listened to more carefully by the mass of peoples; it provided evidence from non-Jewish writings of the epochs and writings of Jews in accordance with their time, and here Gans quoted R. Moses Isserlis in his support; it will recall 'certain celestial signs, new stars and eclipses', showing that these were a portent of earthly happenings; it will inform Jews of the remote past, so that they will be enabled to answer the questions of non-Jews and talk with them 'and find favour in their eyes', and not appear like animals who do not know the difference between their right and their left, 'as though we were all born yesterday'; lastly, history will manifest the existence of kings and emperors so that if we, in our exile, have none, we will be inspired to pray to God, 'to bring back our judges as at the beginning' (Isaiah i, 26).[56]

Gans' history served not only to express the hope but also the reality of a more friendly relationship with the Christian world : his explicit reference to the need for Jews to talk with their Christian neighbours on equal terms and thereby earn their respect; the fact that Part II dealing with the non-Jewish world is much the same length as Part I; that he enumerates and gives references to his Christian sources in the evident expectation that his readers will wish to enquire further – all this supports the suggestion above. Lastly, note Gans' very warm reference to Prague and Bohemia. How appropriately did it choose the lion as its national emblem, he exclaimed. Prague he exalts as 'the great and lively and populous capital' of a country with a multitude of villages, fair places and castles. 'This land is full of the blessing of the Lord', with grain, wine and strong drink (Numbers VI, 3) with its many rivers, forests and pastures, timber in plenty, with deposits of tin at Schalckwald, of silver at Joachimstal and Rothenberg, of mercury, of gold – to say nothing of the hot springs of Karlsbad and Toeplitz, 'than which no travellers have ever told us that better existed'.[57] All this is of a piece with Gans' tendency to omit matters that might disturb relations with the Christian world, e.g. persecutions and disputations, and rather to stress Jewish survival; his neglect of the Jewish mystical tradition lest this dismay the enlightened sixteenth century; and his discreet glorification of Gentile rulers.[58] Noteworthy also is Gans' muted messianism. Whereas, for example, the Turkish capture of Constantinople in 1453 had been a keystone in Abrabanel's schema, Gans merely mentioned the presence of Christians amongst the Turkish forces, eliciting a reference to Isaiah IL, 17; 'Thy destroyers and they that made thee waste shall go forth from thee.'[59]

Of all the developments of the sixteenth century none was more forward-looking than the critical study of sources. This originated, naturally enough, in Italy, where Jewish culture was suffused with Christian elements to a greater extent than elsewhere.[60] The pioneer in Jewish historical thinking of a technique more familiar to Christians was Azariah dei Rossi.

Rossi, a scholar of uncertain occupation, was born in Mantua *c.* 1511. He came of a family that had long associations with the court life of the Gonzaga rulers of the city (the later court musician and composer, Salomone dei Rossi, was a kinsman) and here Rossi received his Jewish and general education. He later lived in various Italian cities – Ferrara, Bologna, Ancona, etc. – depending on the vicissitudes of expulsion. He was about sixty when he returned to Ferrara and wrote *Me'or Eynayim* (Light of the Eyes) which was eventually published in Mantua in 1573. Rossi died *c.* 1578.

Me'or Eynayim is divided into three discrete parts : the first, an account of the author's experiences during the earthquake at Ferrara in 1571; the second, a Hebrew translation of the *Letter of Aristeas*. The fact that this part was undertaken at all confirms the argument of Zacuto and Gans that Jews required greater familiarity with their own past to discuss matters of common interest with enquiring Christians.[61] The apocryphal *Letter*, a piece of Judeo-Hellenistic literature purporting to describe *inter alia* the Temple of Jerusalem and the origin of the Septuagint, was the subject of a question put to Rossi by a Christian scholar (both had taken refuge in the countryside from the earthquake) who wished to know the Hebrew reading at one point in the text. But there was no Hebrew version and Rossi replied that the *Letter* was all but unknown to his fellow-Jews.

The third part of *Me'or Eynayim* is entitled 'Imrei Bina' – Words of Understanding – and is the most important in the present context. It contains Rossi's essays on such topics as the Judeo-Hellenistic writings of Philo of Alexandria (which had been consistently neglected by the rabbis), the source of the Septuagint, the relatively late origin of the Hebrew calendar, the historical value of Midrashic and aggadic literature, and on such antiquities as the vestments worn by the High Priests, the structure of the Temple Service and so on. Rossi brought to his treatment of these and other aspects of the Jewish past not only familiarity with the Jewish sources but also a deep and extensive acquaintance with the non-Jewish – classical, medieval and Renaissance.[62] For his love of books, wide reading and knowledge of the esoteric byways of literature Rossi has been well compared to Montaigne.[63]

When Rossi brought to the study of the Jewish past the humanism of Renaissance Italy and the classical revival, he not only used Gentile sources without the slightest inhibition but he also used them not solely to confirm Jewish tradition – as some previous students had done, e.g. Zacuto (see above p. 41) but, on occasion, also to challenge and even correct tradition. As to the 'calculators of the end', and in explicit reference to the messianologists R. Abraham b. Hiyya and Don Isaac Abrabanel, Rossi forthrightly condemned the 'confusion' of those who 'imagined in their souls to bring to light the hidden with the help of the decrees of the stars and the great conjunctions of the heavenly hosts . . .'[64] This is to say nothing of the way in which Rossi's researches into the history of the Hebrew calendar (that was supposedly coeval with the creation) destroyed the basis for all messianic calculations derived from traditional calendaric data.[65]

Yet Rossi was no *Maskil* of the nineteenth century. His aims were inherently modest in that he directed his research to clarifying certain aspects of tradition, although it was of the essence of Rossi's method that it should in fact enter into matters other than the rabbinic *kabbalah*. This enlarged scope, however, and the comparative method did set Rossi apart from his predecessors and make his work the sole attempt to articulate a more positive and also a more critical stance towards the study of Jewish history until the nineteenth century. *Me'or Eynayim* also stands isolated in the centuries that separate Josephus from Jost in that it reveals a passionate and disinterested love of the past for its own sake and in its own right.

Rossi sought to justify his freedom of approach by making an early reference to the Talmudic tractate *Berakhoth* (63b : 'a man should always first learn *Torah* and then scrutinise it') and to the tractate *Shabbath* (63a : 'that a man should study and subsequently understand'). He added, 'for howsoever we follow the quest for wisdom, benefit may be hoped for, because by way of this study without regard to its type . . . there will not lack a desirable advantage in that, through its strength, we will acquire forces of understanding and, as we have explained, it is in man's nature and sweet to the soul.' He now referred to Cicero who,

> in the third of his speeches and in the fifth of his letters described the reading of different tales a pleasure to the ears and found therefore, that histories which encompass much rise and fall and change will delight and attract their hearers; Quintilianus also, in Book ix, Chapter 1, said that it is in the nature of human beings to delight in change and in Book xi, Chapter 12 wrote that varied study will preserve us from weariness and strengthen the soul.[66]

'Without regard to its type' : this evidently signified the willingness to use Gentile sources. Rossi based himself on Ben Zoma's dictum : 'Who is wise? He who learns from all men. As it is said (Psalms cxix, 99) "from all my teachers I get understanding" ' (*Pirkei Avoth*, iv); also on Jeremiah (xviii, 13) : 'therefore thus saith the Lord : "ask ye now among the nations, who hath heard such things." ' Rossi combined this readiness to use sources 'that are not of our people' with the claim to considerable freedom of interpretation *vis-à-vis* Jewish commentators. He asked whether it was possible 'to doubt and dispute the words of the sages in the interpretation of writings which are in the *Torah* and do not refer to its commandments and similarly with deeds of history that they relate and expound to us – can we say in any aspect that the matter was not so or not at the time that it was said to be . . . ?' To this he replied :

> it is certain that no servitude lies on us and there is no source of suspicion if we differ from them since our words are not against

them in any one of the three principal matters that we shall
speak of in Chapter 28 but each man in accordance with his
understanding and the strength of the evidence that he will
bring to his words is free in speech, save that he must direct his
heart to the truth and the heavens.[67]

Rossi emphasised that

although we wish to acknowledge that some of the tales came to
the ears of our sages with some confusion and thus they related
them to us, this does not detract from their honour . . . but the
beautiful soul will yearn in all things to know its truth . . . and
in any case it is good that the books read amongst us should
not include inaccuracies but only what is established, and
correct writing.[68]

The 'three principal matters' (in Chapter xxvIII) beyond discussion are any matters related in the name of Moses, or derived
from the *Torah* by the accepted hermeneutical rules or made by
the sages into 'a fence round the *Torah*'. But this status, Rossi
continued, could clearly not be enjoyed by matters which 'by their
nature could not possibly have been made known to them at
Sinai, e.g. an account of events between then and now or matters
which are undoubtedly known to have been uttered by them
through the exertion of their soul without the compulsion of
scripture.'[69] As an example of unclarity Rossi cited the differences
in the sources over the identity of the author of a massacre of
Jews in Alexandria : the Jerusalem Talmud gave Traginus, often
referred to in the Midrashim as Tracinus; in Tractate *Sukkah*
the Babylonian Talmud gave Alexander of Macedon; and in the
Tractate *Gittin,* Hadrian. Rossi continued : '. . . we have now
resolved to investigate the correctness of these matters not because
of the fact itself – for what was, was – only because we are
concerned that the words of our sages in narrating noted events
should not contradict each other . . .'[70]

Three ways can be distinguished in which Rossi enlarged the
domain open to critical assessment. First, since this was to some
extent a *querelle des anciens et des modernes,* there was advance-
ment in knowledge – though not of course everywhere. In matters
concerning prophecy, for example, those who came earlier had
the clear advantage over their successors, 'through their greater

closeness to the authors' (of prophecy). But in matters where 'the shoot came from the root of speculation and experiment, thread being forever added to thread and cord to cord . . . ', those who came later benefited clearly over their forerunners.[71] This was exemplified in the progress of astronomy and, at a later stage in his argument, Rossi drew for support on Maimonides. He quoted the 'Guide' (III, 14):

> Do not ask of me to show that everything they [i.e. the sages] have said concerning astronomical matters conforms to the way things really are. For at that time mathematics were imperfect. They did not speak about this as transmitters of the dicta of the prophets, but rather because in those times they were men of knowledge in these fields or because they had heard these dicta from the men of knowledge who lived in those times.[72]

Second, Rossi distinguished between those traditions that came from Sinai or from prophetic sources and those that were the utterances of an individual (possibly mistaken) sage.[73]

Third, he treated the Midrashim and Midrashic elements in general with reserve and criticism, asserting for example that 'they exaggerated in three directions'. He gave examples of rabbinic encounters with fantastic fish (as in *Baba Bathra*, 73b) or of a meeting between R. Bana'ah and Abraham and Adam (ibid., 58a).[74] The most telling example concerned the gnat which, according to the rabbis (e.g. *Gittin*, 56b) entered Titus' nose during his return from Jerusalem to Rome, swelled inside the emperor's brain and eventually caused his death. This was the divine punishment for Titus' destruction of the Temple. But not only were there discrepancies in the rabbinic sources themselves, Rossi argued, not only was the incident medically impossible (with a reference at this point to the French sixteenth-century physician Johannes Fernelius), not only did Titus mount the throne at the very time when, according to the rabbis, he died – apart from all this, Rossi cited eight historians of note who attributed Titus' death to ague: Caesari, Cassiodorus, Hermanus Contractus, Suetonius, Eutropius, Platina, Petrus Mexia seu Messia and Petrarch.[75]

But did this matter? Was it important that the rabbis and sages erred, even perhaps through wilful exaggeration and fancifulness, in historical matters? Moreover, was it not perfectly understandable that those 'who occupy themselves with the *Torah* do not dwell on [historical] errors'?[76] There was of course a general requirement that nothing confused or contradictory should mar rabbinic data. But beyond this . . . ? In the crucial Chapter xxvii of *Imrei Bina*, Rossi expounded the limited importance of history *tel quel* to the Jew, the eminently justifiable inaccuracies or exaggerations of the rabbis and his own limited role as scrutineer of the past.

Rossi began by heaping encomia on Livy, 'the glory and ornament of his native city of Padua', for the hundred and forty volumes of his history 'of the great city of Rome'. He quoted Livy on the lessons that can be learned from chronicles of the past : 'we will recognise what is good for ourselves and for our people, to remove what is harmful and to bring close what is helpful'. But Rossi then made a crucial distinction between the Gentile and Jewish worlds. Whereas Livy's words, he argued, are

> not fallacious in respect of the peoples who have not seen the light of the perfect *Torah* with the other holy writings and work in the darkness of human studies for they, with the sweat of their efforts and exertion of their mind, will have to sift and differentiate everything that the earth produces through the action of men and beasts and consider what good will come to them from their history. But we, the people of the God of Abraham – and the seed that serve Him . . . have already left this task free and upright to the degree that no advantage remains to us if we would trouble ourselves overmuch with this, for with His *Torah* and commandments has He not turned all the darkness before us into light and opened to us the gates of righteousness . . . ?

In this perspective it was quite natural that the rabbis should err – and Rossi heaped reference on reference to justify cavalier rabbinic unconcern with historical fact through their very concentration on the exclusive study of the *Torah* – that 'this book of the Law shall not depart out of thy mouth, but thou shalt meditate therein day and night . . .' (Joshua i, 8); that they reproved those who prayed at the expense of study for 'they forsake eternal life and occupy themselves with temporal life' (*Shabbath*, 10a); that 'one who speaks of profane matters transgresses both a negative and a positive precept' (*Yoma*, 12b); that even in order to rebuild the Temple schoolchildren were forbidden to neglect their studies (*Shabbath*, 119b; *Megila*, 3) etc. Rossi himself commented,

> because of these words whose truth it is precious to us to expound, we should not be surprised if they [i.e. the Talmudic sages] busy themselves and concern themselves with the *Torah* alone, and do not turn to the arrogance of secular discourse and the reading of memorials of what happened at earlier times, so that there goes forth from them some confusion or abbreviation in some story taken from those discourses. For into a matter that does not deceive the sons of men it is not their habit to enquire but to transmit the matter in the form in which they have received it themselves . . .'[77]

To sum up : first, history could teach the Jew nothing, for the *Torah* contained all he needed to know; second, even if the sages had undoubtedly erred in their transmission of fact, or had exaggerated, or distorted events in a fanciful way, this was perfectly excusable, either because such errors were simply inconsequential and immaterial to their teaching – 'what was, was' – or because it testified to their all-consuming devotion to the *Torah* by comparison with which they considered everything else secondary, as did Rossi himself; third, even in this limited context, however, it was incumbent on the student to correct the sages; and, fourth, for this purpose the use of Gentile sources was fully justifiable.

Even this modest and auxiliary purpose did not protect Rossi from censure and attack. At their most severe they came from R. Joseph Caro, the authoritative codifier (*Shulhan Arukh*, 1564–5). Caro had a decree prepared calling for the burning of *Me'or Eynayim*, but he died before he could sign it.[78] The Italian rabbinical authorities in such centres as Venice, Pesaro, Ancona, Rome, Verona, Pedua, Ferrara, Siena, etc. were less extreme : they did not suppress the book but required intending readers to obtain special permission from the local rabbinate.[79] Despite these precautions the book was already making its mark on Rossi's contemporaries. Gans, for example, in his history, made repeated reference to Rossi though he did so without mentioning the author's name.[80]

From the Maharal of Prague came the most reasoned opposi-

c

tion. The Maharal was no opponent on principle of secular studies but he did indeed attack those who, as he saw it, confused the study of philosophy and mysticism (such as his contemporaries, R. Moses Isserlis and R. Eliezer Ashkenazi) or those (such as Levi ben Gersonides of an earlier generation) who brought to the study of miracles a rationalist classification into miracles of substance (e.g. when Moses's staff turned into a serpent or the river Nile to blood) and miracles of accident (when the hand of Moses became leprous).[81]

In the case of Rossi, at first the Maharal proposed, in a Solomonic spirit, 'not to answer a fool according to his folly' (Proverbs xxvi, 4). But then, seeing *Me'or Eynayim* in print and reaching the many, he followed the contrary injunction of Solomon – 'answer a fool according to his folly' (Ibid., 5).[82] He saw 'this man [Rossi] seducing . . . the masses'.[83]

The wide range of the Maharal's defence of the aggadic elements in Talmud and Midrash far surpassed the relatively narrow limits of his counter-attack against Rossi.[84] But within those limits he proclaimed the superior wisdom of the earlier sages against the later,[85] whereas Rossi had echoed the dictum that though we may be pygmies, at least we are pygmies on the shoulders of giants in relation to matters dependent on experiment.[86] The Maharal particularly contested Rossi's view of the Aggadah, ascribing to Rossi the view that these were 'only cunning words to attract men's hearts with cords of falsehood'.[87] On the contrary, the Aggadah concealed an esoteric wisdom, and what to Rossi were literary conceits or devices, signified to the Maharal the language of mystical enlightenment. Underlying this view was the Maharal's belief in the existence of two orders of reality, as it were – the natural and the divine. In the same way as there was 'a customary order to the world of nature according to its nature so there was also an order to the miracles'.[88] The former depended on the latter, the divine order, for this was 'the cause of the cause', and it was of this that the sages spoke : 'the sages did not come to speak of a natural cause, small and petty as it is, for this is appropriate to those versed in nature or to doctors but not to sages who spoke of the cause which determines nature.'[89] The gravamen of the Maharal's counter-attack against Rossi's criticism was grounded in the latter's wilful confusion of two levels of discourse and understanding; the divine and the natural, to say nothing of the fact that he had brought secular, non-Jewish, sources into play. Rossi had used methods appropriate to one order of reality as a means to elucidate another and totally different order.[90]

Thus the Maharal denied that natural causes could in any way explain the rainbow mentioned in Genesis ix, 12–17; or, if the sages had declared that the size of the world was six thousand *parasangs,* 'do not allow yourself to think that this magnitude was presented as though it were measured by material measurement'. The number six, argued the Maharel, 'has the essence of completion . . . for every body has six sides and therefore if the world is said to be six thousand *parasangs* the intention is to show that the world is complete in itself . . .'; on similar lines, the Maharal argued that the land of Israel lay at the centre of the earth, 'in the same way as the navel is man's centre . . . If you measure with a line the navel is not the centre in terms of physical measurement but it does lie mid-way between what is known as the upper part and the lower part . . .'[91]

As for the gnat that entered Titus' nose, the Maharal emphasised more vigorously than ever before that the sages did not concern themselves with 'revealed material matters', and a proof brought from nature has no relevance to a miracle. Rather, 'the meaning is that any creature has a specific essence by virtue of which, it is what it is.' With the gnat an 'active force' entered the brain of Titus, the essence of the gnat. The Maharal denied that this explanation departed from the 'plain meaning' of the text, for the sages had precisely in mind such a blow as would explain the action of Titus. 'The principle of the matter is to show that because Titus destroyed the House of our Lord by means of which Israel was bound to their father in heaven', the blow that struck him was 'a force that splits and divides'.[92]

The Maharal fought off Rossi's attack. It was not renewed until the nineteenth century, although Rossi's work was indeed referred to in the meantime, becoming known to the non-Jewish world of scholarship (through Latin translations of extracts) and to such Biblical scholars as Richard Simon and Buxtorf.[93] Zunz did not err when he called Rossi 'the first man who taught Israel the science of research which is the basis of scholarship'.[94] But when Rossi's naturalistic sobriety and critico-comparative approach were renewed in the nineteenth century, they had lost their contact with the world of *praxis* and become academic. They were no longer an auxiliary to the study of the tradition of the *Kabbalah*. Rossi's successors of the nineteenth century did not write in order to expunge error but pursued their study for its own sake.

5 The Decline of the Messiah

Probably the last attempt to construct a Jewish history in terms of rabbinic scholarship came from R. Yehiel Halperin of Minsk. His *Seder Ha'Dorot* (Order of the Generations, 1769) is precisely such a work. He saw himself in the same tradition as Zacuto and Ibn Yahya. Indeed, he castigated them for their defective presentative of the *Kabbalah*, whilst giving qualified praise to Gans. The ignorance of his own generation appalled Halperin. He emphasised that 'a knowledge of the generations' will show who is the teacher and who the pupil – following the precedent established by Maimonides and Alfassi. 'In this way you will be able to understand how to correct many errors in the Talmud and you will find hundreds that need correction.' Halperin undertook to cite 'two great men who erred because of their defective knowledge of the sequence of the generations'.[1]

This was the swan-song of the *Kabbalah*. The interest earlier shown in extra-legal studies by the Prague circle of the Maharal, by the Italian Jews, by the Poles, to say nothing of the Jews of Spain, took on wider dimensions. In his autobiography, for example, the noted scholar of the eighteenth century, R. Jacob Emden (1697–1776), deplored his ignorance of foreign languages and foreign literatures – which however, Emden subsequently overcame – and yearned to know something of 'the peoples and their beliefs and their attributes and their opinions and their history and their sciences . . . the laws of each state and the nature of the lands and of the inhabitants, to uncover their secrets . . . but I was careful not to read and glance at works on these subjects except where it was forbidden to meditate on the words of the *Torah*.'[2]

This mood expressed a *rapprochement* with the world of European letters, which, in respect of historiography, initiated a partial transformation of the dominant tradition. When two historians of the twentieth century – Isaac Baer and Israel Rabin – looked back to the eighteenth, they saw the emergence of modern Jewish historiography as part and parcel of what the latter termed the Jewish entry 'into the world of European culture'.[3]

History of the rabbinic tradition conceived as such lost its *raison d'être* for two clear, not necessarily related, reasons : first, the decline of the will to separate existence on the part of the Jewish communities amidst emancipation, or at least growing tolerance; second, the political reality of the corporate state of the *ancien régime,* with its encouragement of Jewish autonomy, yielded to a system that gradually destroyed that autonomy, together with its legal sanctions, institutions and so on, in the interest of the legal equality of all citizens.[4] Part of the Jewish recognition of this changing situation was formulated by Moses Mendelssohn whose 'Jerusalem' (1783) brought the Jew within the orbit of the Christian state and sought to diminish the powers of the rabbinate.[5] This policy abruptly reversed the earlier Jewish insistence on the preservation of internal autonomy.

Another victim of this new order was the messiah. In western Jewish circles this lost its Israel-centredness, and that aspect which had always referred to 'the nations of the world' began to overshadow the rest. The perennial tension was obscured in favour of a universalist abstraction.

The sociological study of Jewish messianism has been neglected by comparison with the abundant study of Utopian and millenial thought in the Gentile world so that it is impossible to define the precise circumstances in which messianic convictions and activities flourished. But a certain degree of stability and prosperity clearly had a strongly debilitating effect. In Poland, for example in the early seventeenth century, certain moralists and preachers deplored the lack of interest that the wealthy showed in redemption. 'Far from them is the search for salvation.' Their wealth made the Diaspora dear to them.[6] Similarly, in England in the early nineteenth century, Macaulay rightly compared the intensity of the Christian and Jewish beliefs in redemption :

> Does a Jew engage less eagerly than a Christian in any competition which the law leaves open to him? . . . Does he furnish his house meanly, because he is a pilgrim and sojourner in the

land? Does the expectation of being restored to the country of his fathers make him insensible to the fluctuations of the stock exchange? Does he, in arranging his private affairs, ever take into account the chance of his migrating to Palestine?[7]

Three decades earlier or so the Napoleonic campaign in Egypt and Palestine, the later convocation of a Sanhedrin in Paris (1807) and the invasion of eastern Europe did indeed suggest to some observers in the Hassidic and rabbinic courts of Poland and Galicia the wars of Gog and Magog and messianic imminence. But opinions were divided. Whereas R. Menachem Mendel of Rimanov prayed for Napoleon's victory, 'so that redemption would come', the Seer of Lublin argued that the time of redemption was not yet ripe and prayed for Napoleon's defeat.[8] From New York, perhaps, came the most forthright anticipation – in a sermon delivered by the Reverend Gershom Seixas on 11 January 1807:

among the many events predicted by the Prophets to take place previous to restoration of Israel, to their former glory and pre-eminence, the convocation of our brethren in Zarephath [i.e. France] may be viewed as one of not the least extraordinary, for under the auspices of the most powerful potentate of Europe and after the lapse of seventeen centuries since our captivity, he has collected the most learned of our Rabbanim who reside in his dominions, and invited everyone who incline to attend from other countries, to assemble in his metropolis, to form a Sanhedrin; let us pray that the God of Israel may so direct them . . . that they may find favour in the sight of their Emperor, and that he, under the influence of divine grace, may be a means to accomplish our re-establishment, if not as a nation in our former territory, let it only be as a particular society, with equal rights and privileges of all other religious societies.[9]

But all this was but a shadow of earlier anticipations. It seems indeed as though Protestant restorationist thought flowed more enthusiastically than Jewish.[10]

In modern times, the first steps towards a redefinition and devitalisation of the messianic concept were taken in Germany. This responded both to the acceptance of the authority of the state by the Jewish community and to the prevalence of universalist ideals in Europe generally. A correspondingly universalist emphasis came to characterise the messianic idea.[11] Worse came in the 1830s and 1840s when the rabbinical conferences of Brunswick, Frankfurt and Breslau rejected the idea of Jewish nationhood and emphasised to the exclusion of all else the spiritual aspect of the messiah, in part identifying it with the improved civil and political status of the Jews.[12] The new messianic theories became all but indistinguishable from the ideology of progress. Hermann Cohen at the beginning of the twentieth century removed the idea from its *halakhic* base and transformed it into a purely theoretical vision of the future universal union of mankind, destined to annihilate past and present and overcome the separate existence of men and peoples, 'in this existence of the future'.[13] He even saw 'the state before our eyes ripening into a League of Nations. Messianism is becoming a factor in world history'.[14]

Towards the end of the eighteenth century, when this whole process began, the immediate effect was to make possible the study of Jewish history in terms that approximated to those prevalent in Gentile historiography. This was inevitable. If it is true that the historical content and nature of Judaism completely replaced the need for conventional historical study then, with the reformulation of Judaism, and particularly of such a crucial historical component as the messiah, a new historiography *à l'européenne* must emerge. The messianic idea was as much political as anything else, in the sense that it included the restoration of Israel to the Land of Israel. Therefore, if this component of the idea fell away or was redefined in terms that were less uncompromisingly historical – then a whole historical schema must suffer.

This must be all the more so if a previous staple theme of historical writing – the rabbinic tradition – was fast advancing towards the loss of its practical relevance and internal strength.[15] As the Jew, at least in parts of central and western Europe, became a citizen of the appropriate state, his hitherto undivided attachment became fragmented to such effect that historiography became necessary as a means to the restoration of unity. But most of all, it was perhaps diminution in the credibility of the messiah that created the need for history. As the messiah departed, Clio entered, but in Jewish garb.

The initial perplexity and part of its resolution can be exemplified in the reaction of Moses Mendelssohn to the new circumstances of Jewish existence. Mendelssohn was temperamentally averse to historical study. 'What do I know of history?' he asked; '. . . I always yawn when I must read something historical', he wrote to his friend Thomas Abbt.[16] Philosophically also, Mendelssohn belonged to that rationalist, anti-historical lineage epitomised in the views of Aristotle, Descartes, etc.[17] In the variegated, tumultuous world of historical events he could not see a reliable fund or certain content of knowledge. For Mendelssohn the truth of Judaism was contained in the universal principles of reason that it enunciated.[18]

But this did not fully accommodate the ambiguous position in which Mendelssohn found himself. It was not dissimilar to that described by young Hegel in respect of the Germans. Who am I? Who are my models?[19] For the Jews this was a measure of the confusion brought by the enlightenment, Jewish and non-Jewish. When Abbt enquired as to 'the attribute' of Mendelssohn's 'fellow-countrymen', Mendelssohn asked: 'Of which fellow-countrymen? the Dessauer? Or the citizen of Jerusalem?'[20] This ambiguity was necessarily reflected in Mendelssohn's attitude *vis-à-vis* the world of history. He wrote to Abbt: 'I have hitherto considered history more for the knowledge of the citizen [citoyen] than of the man; and believed that a man who has no country could promise himself no benefit from history.'[21]

If there was no room for the Jew within the history of a state, then did universal history offer accommodation? Mendelssohn does seem to suggest that since 'the history of civil constitution and the history of mankind flow into one another', this might offer a solution.[22] But the appearance of the universalist work of even so well-intentioned an *Aufklärer* as Lessing showed this hope to be an illusion. Lessing's *Erziehung des Menschengeschlechts* with its idea of progress could not but be unacceptable to an observant Jew such as Mendelssohn.[23]

Given the weakening of the old messianic conviction – given, also, the evident incapacity of existing historiography to accommodate the Jew – the only recourse was to create a Jewish historiography. This would seek to repair the partial breach created through the loss of the messianic schema. It would seek to replace the historical framework, now damaged through the eclipse of

c*

the messiah, by varied historical frameworks each of which, even while absorbing its measure of non-Jewish influence, did carry over into the new era many of the traditional ideas. All but irretrievably lost was the notion of Jewish history as that of the *Kabbalah.*

It was symptomatic of the new status accorded to the study of Jewish history that it came to be seen not only as a necessity but also as the vehicle to introduce the Jewish enlightenment of Germany to eastern European Jewry. For example, Mendelssohn and a group of his followers planned to commission Solomon Maimon to prepare a translation of Basnage's *L'Histoire et la Religion des Juifs* (5 vols, 1706–11).[24] The project proved abortive but the persistent relevance of the idea can be seen in the campaign of Naftali Herz Weisl to spread secular knowledge amongst Jews. He sought to show the importance of history as a means to the understanding of Scripture and argued that the student should learn 'how kingdoms were founded and the names of the peoples who took territories the one from the other to this day, what were their leaders, their deeds, their laws, for this knowledge helps us to understand the words of the *Torah* . . . and he who is not versed in the narrations of early times, all these matters are to him as a dream without an interpretation.'[25] Note also the publication by the journals *Me'assef* and *Sulamit* of biographies of such historical personages as Don Isaac Abrabanel and R. Menasseh b. Israel; the historical writings of Peter Beer and S. Levisohn; and the multitude of studies devoted to virtually all components of the Jewish past by scholars in central and eastern Europe. This paralleled the historical ferment in the non-Jewish world.[26]

Amongst the first fruits of the new world were the historical studies of Issac Marcus Jost (1798–1860), who fully affirmed the need to diminish Jewish separatism, welcomed the new opportunities presented by emancipation and sought to 'mediate between Synagogue and world culture'.[27] Far more significant was the movement known as *die Wissenschaft des Judentums* – the Science of Judaism. This was the creation of a group of young German-Jewish intellectuals centred on Berlin and its university in the early decades of the nineteenth century.[28]

The movement enunciated the principles of a vast movement of scholarship that would dominate the nineteenth century and survive into the twentieth. Its Manifesto, published in 1822, was the work of Immanuel Wolf (Wohlwill), a graduate in philosophy of the Universities of Berlin and Kiel. By Judaism the Manifesto understood 'the essence of all the circumstances, characteristics and achievements of the Jews in relation to religion, philosophy, history, law, literature in general, civil life and all the affairs of men.' Although the Jews now lived in isolation, 'in peaceful brooding over the letters of vanished centuries', Judaism had for most of the world's history shown itself to be 'an important and influential factor in the development of the human spirit.' Now, with 'the irresistible progress of spirit' and the cessation of 'extreme pressure', the time had come, Wolf argued, to treat Judaism 'scientifically'. By this he meant 'the systematic unfolding and re-presentation of its object in its whole sweep, for its own sake, and not for any ulterior purpose . . . unfolding Judaism in accordance with its essence . . . it begins without any preconceived opinion and is not concerned with the final result.'[29]

The work of Leopold Zunz, the outstanding scholar of the *Wissenschaft des Judentums*, best embodied this ideal. Zunz was born in 1794 in Detmold, attended the *Gymnasium* in Wolfenbüttel (the first Jewish pupil to do so) and entered the University of Berlin in 1815. Here he came under the influence of the great philologists and classical scholars, Friedrich August Wolf and August Böckh – perhaps also the influence of Savigny and Alexander v. Humboldt.[30]

Zunz saw the Jewish past in terms of a literature that most adequately expressed the spirit of Judaism.[31] He also had plans for the collection of statistics relating to the contemporary Jewish world that would be equivalent to a sociology. But it was to the study of literature in the widest sense that Zunz dedicated himself – in the comprehensive sense in which this was understood by the Berlin school of philology and history.[32] His first work – *Etwas über die rabbinische Literatur* (Berlin, 1818) already announced a programme conceived in this spirit, embracing theology, poetry, law, homiletics, etc. as literature. This would not only serve apologetic purposes in revealing the nature and extent of Jewish intellectual activity, and by this token argue in favour of further political advance, but also provide a fitting conclusion to an activity for which Zunz at that time saw no future. He was the owl of Minerva taking wing in the twilight of post-Biblical Hebrew literature : 'precisely because we see the Jews in our day . . . carrying neo-Hebrew literature to its grave, science arises and demands a settlement of that which is concluded' (*Rechenschaft von der geschlossenen*).[33]

But the truly revolutionary element in Zunz's programme, and generally in that of the *Wissenschaft des Judentums*, was the notion of Jewish literature as a creation to stand alongside that of others in the total creativity of humanity. This automatically removed, not its uniqueness, but the unique role hitherto attributed to that literature as a continuing effort to elucidate and implement a particular divine revelation. Judaism came to be regarded no longer as the pivot of world history but suffered a degradation of status to become one voice amongst the many that together made up 'the human spirit'. Closely allied to the degradation of Judaism was its reduction to the level of *belles-lettres*. The aesthetic motif that had made a first fleeting appearance in David's association of 'statutes' with 'songs' (Psalms cxix, 54 : see above p. 15), i.e. the separation of theory and practice, made its reappearance by way of historical research. In his essay on rabbinic literature Zunz expressed the belief that 'our science is to . . . emancipate itself from the theologians and rise to the historical viewpoint' :[34] 'we are not afraid of being misunderstood. Here the whole literature of the Jews, in its widest context, is presented as an object for research, without our being concerned whether its total content also should or can be a norm for our own judgement.'[35] That object of research was no longer a means to the further exposition of the past with a view to the emulation or extension or clarification of the tradition, but study for the pure sake of study. R. Hiyya (fourth century) and R. Aha (second century) bring out the full force of this innovation. The first said : 'If a man learns the Law without intending to fulfil that Law, it were better for him had he never been born.' On the contrary, argued the latter, 'he who learns in order to do is worthy to receive the Holy Spirit.'[36]

But the new learning introduced a divorce into the traditional union of thought and action, theory and practice. The new historical techniques secularised study[37] and this was tantamount to its devitalisation.

The Jewish past thus faced the danger of degenerating into the 'picture gallery' that Nietzsche held up as a threat to life. 'A historical phenomenon, purely and completely understood and dissolved into a phenomenon of cognition is, for he who has cognized it, dead . . . History conceived as pure science and become sovereign would be a sort of life-conclusion and a settlement of account for mankind.' (*Vom Nutzen und Nachteil der Historie für das Leben*, I)[38]

The threat to Judaism of the consequences of a historical consciousness of this type was recognised early in the nineteenth century. At one extreme it was denounced by S. D. Luzzatto who, in 1847, accused the followers of the Science of Judaism of holding Goethe and Schiller in greater esteem than all the prophets, *Tannaim* and *Amoraim*; for love of glory they investigated Israel's past as others investigated the past of Assyria, Egypt, Babylon and Persia.[39] The rationalist commitment of these writers and their undisguised quest for political emancipation compounded this noxious outlook in Luzzatto's eyes.[40] But it was Samson Raphael Hirsch who drew the full consequences :

> Moses and Hesiod, David and Sappho, Deborah and Tyrtaeus, Isaiah and Homer, Delphi and Jerusalem, Pythian tripod and Cherubim-sanctuary, prophets and oracles, psalms and elegy – for us they all lie peacefully in one box, they all rest peacefully in one grave, they all have one and the same human origin, they all have one and the same significance, human, transitory, and belonging to the past. All the clouds have dispersed. The tears and sighs of our fathers fill no longer our hearts, but our *libraries*. The warmly pulsating hearts of our fathers has become our national *literature*, their fervent breath of life has become the dust of bookshelves. We let the old Jews fast on *Tisha B'Av*, we let them say *Selichot* and weep over *Kinot*. But in return we know far better than they do in which century these "poets" flourished, in what metre these poets "composed", who it was that nursed them when they were infants. . . . Do these departed spirits rejoice in the literary gratitude of our present generation? Whom do they recognize as their true heirs? Those who repeated their prayers, but forgot their names, or those who forget their prayers but remember their names?[41]

Despite the forebodings of Hirsch and Luzzatto, the challenge presented by at least certain representatives of the Science of Judaism did not go unanswered, even in that science's own terms.

It proved possible to use the critical methods developed and proclaimed by the Science, but to contrary ends, rehabilitating Judaism as an entity that did not belong irretrievably to the past as an object of study. Judaism, paradoxically, was validated in terms of history despite, or perhaps because of, history. Precisely through the historical-mindedness of the nineteenth century, the historian of Israel would seek to preserve its uniqueness – not, indeed, through the authority of the *Kabbalah* but through the notion of a distinct and exemplary destiny, as much in the present as in the past. In the work of R. Nahman Krochmal, Graetz and Dubnow, themes from the messianic past remained dominant, though in the guise of an immanent historical process.

6 The Messiah as the Spirit of History: Krochmal and Graetz

It has been said: 'What is remarkable is the persistence of historistic-theological thinking among twentieth-century Jewish historians of the Jews, long after Protestant theological methods transcended historicism and developed quite new issues and questions.'[1] This persistence is to be understood as a continuation into modern times of the unending quest for a historical consummation. But the ancient motif was married to the terminology and thought-world of the nineteenth century, and particularly to Hegel and Hegelianism. Whatever the precise degree of dependence between the old and the new, the old stands out within a modern garb, in so far as the messianic idea is assimilated to the supposed movement of history. In modern times this first made itself evident in the work of Krochmal and Graetz. Neither, as traditionally observant and devout Jews, could be a Hegelian, for both must reject the Hegelian notion that the Idea in its various phases was successively embodied in different peoples or worlds, with Judaism relegated to a passing phase of the 'Oriental world'.[2] On the other hand the philosophy of the spirit admirably lent itself to re-formulation in terms that duly acknowledged the centrality of the 'spirit' of Israel.

Krochmal was born in Brody (Galicia) in 1785. He married at the age of fourteen, and became a rabbi in Zolkiev. He died in Tarnopol in 1840. Krochmal, termed by Graetz 'the Polish Mendelssohn',[3] lived far from the centres of the Jewish enlightenment in Germany, though he did maintain close and sometimes personal contact with its representatives in eastern Europe. In matters of modern philosophy he was self-taught. His reading was of the widest – not only the Jewish legal and philosophical and mystical classics but also Rossi, Spinoza, Kant, Horace, Lucianos, etc.[4]

Krochmal's only (and unfinished) work was published posthumously by Zunz (Lemberg, 1851) under the title *Moreh Nevuche Ha'Zman* (Guide to the Perplexed of the Time).[5] There is a strong pedagogic and exhortatory note to his writings. In a reply to the anti-rationalist attacks of Luzzatto, Krochmal saw no distinction between 'a refined faith' and 'the Science of Judaism'.[6] Krochmal set out to provide for his generation the same clarification that Maimonides had given to *his*, some seven centuries earlier :

> to make peace between reason and the written and oral Laws . . . This is the great need in our time . . . in truth our object is like that of Maimonides in the 'Guide' for the people of his time and we always follow in his footsteps in the path of investigation with no other distinction than that between the people of his generation and their perplexity and its necessary cure, and the present generation and its condition.[7]

The difference is of course that whereas Maimonides resolved the perplexity of the twelfth-century Jew in terms of a philosophical restatement of Judaism, Krochmal worked in the medium of history. 'Know yourself' was his motto.[8] This meant the scrutiny of sources, the establishment of a correct chronology, the empirical understanding of providence, the identification of authors, etc. The demand of the present is 'to examine, to investigate and to establish each matter in the true time of its composition.'[9] This was a refrain from Krochmal.[10]

In his uninhibited treatment of the *aggada* he enjoyed a critical freedom that Rossi had pioneered; he felt himself less free in *halakhic* matters; was cautious in matters relating to the Prophets and Hagiographa; and traditional in regard to the Pentateuch.[11] Within these limitations, however, Krochmal did approach a relativistic position and scorned those who took 'individual opinions of a specific time for permanent and eternal truths'.[12]

Graetz, born in Poznan in 1817, knew little of these struggles. By the time of his generation the struggle for a rightful historical method had been won. In his early youth, Graetz combined rabbinic studies with wide reading in modern French and German literature and the Latin classics. He later studied with Samson Raphael Hirsch at Oldenburg; then, by special permission, at the University of Breslau where he was exposed to the Hegelian teaching of Professor Julius Braniss.[13] His doctoral dissertation was presented to the University of Jena and published under the title *Gnostizismus und Judentum* (1846). In later years Graetz lectured in Jewish history and Bible at the Jewish Theological Seminary in Breslau (founded in 1854) and in 1869 was appointed honorary professor at the University of Breslau. Volume four, the first to be published of his *Geschichte der Juden von den ältesten Zeiten bis zur Gegenwart*, appeared in 1853. The remaining ten volumes appeared between 1856 and 1876. Volume eleven (1870) was the occasion for Graetz's polemic of 1879–80 with the German historian Treitschke, who accused Graetz of fostering hostility to Christianity, lacking in German patriotism, adulterating German culture, impeding Jewish assimilation, etc.[14]

There was some sort of parallel in the Jewish world to this controversy. When the Deutsch-Israelitischer-Gemeindebund instituted a 'Historical commission for the history of the Jews in Germany' (1885) to publish documents on German-Jewish history, Graetz was not invited to participate.[15] Similarly, Hermann Cohen included Graetz amongst 'the party of the Palestinians . . . [who have] no roots within German culture'.[16]

Cohen later mellowed.[17] Even so the two men always remained divided through Cohen's insistence on the religious character of Judaism as against Graetz's view that Judaism required the unity of people, land and *Torah* for the realisation of its messianic aim.[18] But that 'nationalist' emphasis which offended large numbers of Graetz's German-Jewish contemporaries was for certain Russian Jews decidedly not nationalist enough. Dubnow, for example, reproached Graetz, in relation to his defence against Treitschke, for his lack of 'a clearly elaborated and fully matured national ideology that he could have set against the firm and rounded system of assimilation. Indeed Graetz was far from claiming the state's recognition of the national rights of the Jewish people, a demand to which only the nationally minded spokesmen of later generations were emboldened, and, moreover, outside the frontiers of Germany.'[19]

This judgement is unfair. It fails to take account of the situation of German Jewry in conditions of emancipation. More important, it lacks recognition of the part that Graetz attributed to the Jew and Judaism in the history of mankind. Graetz identified in the 'idea' of Judaism a messianic promise and reality that made this idea a universal exemplar.

As a historian, Graetz emphatically brought together the two basic themes in Jewish writing about the past : on the one hand, the history of thought and ideas; on the other, the history of suffering and martyrdom. Graetz's work makes a blend of these two traditional 'models' – of, say, Ibn Verga's *Shevet Yehuda* and a history of the *Kabbalah*.

The dual approach was present from the outset. The first published volume (IV, 1853) which treats of the collapse of the Jewish state to the completion of the Talmud (*c.* 500 C.E.), inaugurates the study of the Diaspora under the double aspect of suffering and thought. It also illustrates and exemplifies Graetz's identification of self and subject :

> On the one hand enslaved Judah with his wanderer's staff in hand, the pilgrim's bundle on his back, his grim features turned heavenwards, surrounded by dungeon walls, instruments of torture and the glow of branding irons; on the other, the same figure with a questing look in the transfigured features, in a study filled with a vast library in all the languages of man . . . a slave with a thinker's pride.

The history of suffering is the external history of the Jews : their inner history is the history of thought. 'To seek and to wander, to think and to endure, to learn and to suffer take up the long span of this epoch' (of the Diaspora).[20] With this as his *point de départ*, Graetz then sub-divided the diaspora period into markedly religio-spiritual chronological categories : first, the foundation of the Sanhedrin and school in Yavneh to the collapse of the Gaonate and the Babylonian schools (70–1040); the foundation of the rabbinical schools in Spain to the split between *Denkgläubigkeit* and *Stockgläubigkeit* (1040–1230); the struggle for free enquiry against the rabbinic one-sidedness to the beginning of the new period under Mendelssohn (1230–1780).[21] The period subsequent to Mendelssohn is that of 'growing self-consciousness' – the sub-title to Volume XI.

This subject-matter, limited though it might appear, and despite all 'lachrymose' strictures, none the less enabled Graetz to create a historical structure that would do justice to at least some of the more important components of Jewish experience.

Krochmal, on the other hand, was decidedly less empirical and more rationalist in his procedure. The way to truth, even historical truth, Krochmal affirmed, lay through a process of conceptualisation away from sense impressions. He distrusted, despised even, what he called 'images of the beginning of thought', whereas 'the activity of reason [was] to negate by its reasoning power the details of sense perception, which reveal particular accidents disunited from the general . . .'[22] Krochmal argued that 'the truth of the existence of any matter is not as it appears to the senses but according to its conceptualization in the mind and that a general concept of each and every thing is alone the truth of its existence.'[23]

Hence, when it came to historical methodology Krochmal sought to raise history from the level of detail to that of conceptualisation. In this way the totality of history would be made manifest. He wrote at one point, for example, 'our intention in this chapter is not to examine the details of our history but to elucidate its totality'.[24] The deliberate neglect of detail was again emphasised when Krochmal declared that the particular activities of Johanan Hyrkanos could be found in the histories of the Jews – 'but we will here only clarify what for us is the main thing, all that happened in his days in matters of religion and faith and reforms and the movement of the spirit in general'.[25] This process paralleled Krochmal's understanding of the methodology of Talmudic discussion and legislative activity : the quest for definitions, first principles and categories, etc. as derived by hermeneutical abstraction from particular circumstances.[26]

Krochmal's criticism of Flavius Josephus as a historian who 'recounts events' but only politically', and, 'whilst making known the materiality of many events said hardly anything of the motive spirit that brought them to actuality',[27] is a negative guide to what Krochmal himself looked for in historiography – the movement of the spirit.

This gave Krochmal a positive attitude to the historical process in which reason and progress prevailed, though the latter was by no means uninterrupted. Yet even regression and irrationality could be accounted for, when properly located in the general scheme of things.

Historical movement is the product of men acting in groups. The innate sociable nature of man proclaimed by Krochmal affiliated him to Vico, with whose *Scienza Nuova* (first German translation, Leipzig, 1822) he may well have been familiar, either directly, or indirectly as mediated through Hamann and Herder, with whom Krochmal was certainly familiar. In any case, there is on occasion a close similarity, if not identity, of expression between Vico and Krochmal.[28] But whatever conclusions may or may not be drawn from this, in general the notion of a people as the unit of history was integral to Krochmal's historical scheme. More basic, and in keeping with the principle of conceptualisation, was the notion of a people as embodied in a particular spirit which the particular people both cognised and expressed. Man is a social creature, and when a certain stage in social cohesion is reached, or perhaps through the influence of outsiders, a people comes into being.

In keeping with the doctrine of Vico and Herder, Krochmal regarded a 'people' as a biologico-organic entity. Providence did not scatter man as an isolated individual but in family groupings that developed into clans, cities and political collectives until the stage of 'a complete people' is reached, known as 'a nation and state'. This illustrated Deuteronomy xxxii, 8 : 'When the Most High gave to the nations their inheritance, when He separated the children of men'. Within these collectives useful crafts emerge, legal practices and general ideas. Bonds of love, mutual respect and so on, going beyond the strict requirements of the law, distinguish the community; artistry, music, advance beyond the level of the utilitarian, and all the while sparks of the knowledge of the divine are stirring. There is an enrichment of language, the establishment of schools, the rise of the sciences and a refinement of political and legal systems. These attributes emerged, according to Krochmal, in each people, over a prolonged period and amidst the many, generation after generation. 'These fine inheritances are sometimes born amongst the generality of a people solely over a long period of time, and sometimes by the aid of one tribe which for some reason has reached a higher degree, and sometimes by the aid of groups or individuals who entered it from another land and instructed it and became princes of God and holy leaders like Abraham our father and Melchizedek' (referred to in Genesis xiv, 18 as 'priest of God the Most High').[29]

Those attributes which together made up the spirit of a people were different in quantity but their quality was equal. Thus although each people will differ from its neighbours by virtue of the varying quantities of the various attributes that come together to form its spirit, 'because there is one principle and root to all [attributes] which is the spirit in the people passing from potentiality to actuality . . . then the quality of the attributes will be equal and uniform.' Moreover, in each spirit there will be a harmony amongst its components so that the images of beauty, for example, will accord with those of ethical principles.[30] In other words, the spirit of each people is formed of varying amounts of the same kind of thing.

This individual spirit showed itself to be at work not only in the history of an individual people but also in laws, ethics, religion, language, etc. These are all phenomena in which the spirit of a people is manifested and materialised. It was for this reason that Krochmal could write that 'the essence of a people is not in it in so far as it is a people but in the essence of the spirit within it'. There is a multitude of such spirits but in any individual one that particular attribute will tend to predominate that corresponds to the attitudes present in a particular people. The spirit of bravery, for example, will form the dominant part of the spirit of a people that rules by the sword.[31] Other attributes will only be present in a subordinate capacity.

Each nation's spirit is not wholly immortal – indeed it seems that its decay must inevitably follow the initial period of growth and efflorescence. The stigmata of decay are love of glory, love of pleasure, subjection of thought to the senses, lack of respect for the aged, destruction of the spirit of justice, the use of soothsaying, sorcery to divine the future: 'in short, pleasure, pride, and authority and vain belief, they are the four evil judges that destroy the spirit of the people before it is finished body and soul, internally and externally, and it ceases to be still a people.' But only in so far as spirit is attached to a time and place does it perish when its people perishes. Its innate part, if it is a great people, will attach itself to a neighbouring people, when its own character in the form of poetry, thought and so on will 'become the inheritance of the whole of mankind and the universal spirit'.[32]

If the notion of a *Volksgeist* in the manner of the eighteenth or early nineteenth centuries (Herder, Montesquieu and German idealism) is clearly discernible in Krochmal's doctrine of the 'spirit of a people' and its evanescent nature as expressed in a cycle of formation, maturity and decay,[33] it is also noteworthy that Krochmal himself saw his doctrine in Biblical terms which he then identified with that of his contemporaries. He saw their theories anticipated in such scriptural expressions as spirit of grace and splendour, of judgement and righteousness, of strength, courage, goodness, wisdom, fear of the Lord, etc. : 'of each of these it is said – so-and-so was full of the spirit of the Lord, or the Lord placed His spirit on him, or His spirit rested on him or clothed him. Likewise, amongst later scholars the totality of the spiritual treasure, qualitatively unique and different in each people, is called the spirit of that people in its wholeness.'[34]

Krochmal exemplified and reinforced his analogical interpretation with multiple Biblical references identifying spirit and a people's god, for example : 'And against all the gods of Egypt I will execute judgements' (Exodus xii, 12); 'Behold, I will punish Amon of No, and Pharaoh, and Egypt, with her gods and her kings' (Jeremiah xlvi, 25).[35] He referred also to numerous expressions that spoke of the existence of a multitude of gods : 'foreign gods of the land' (Deuteronomy xxxi, 16); 'gods that they knew not, and that He had not allotted unto them' (Deuteronomy xxix, 25); 'hath a nation changed its gods' (Jeremiah ii, 11); 'for let all the peoples walk each one in the name of its god . . .' (Micah iv, 5).[36] This is how Krochmal would have understood the Midrashic saying : 'God does not punish a people until he has first punished its god.'[37]

The purport of this ancestry becomes particularly evident when Krochmal introduces the God of Israel. Here there is a qualitative distinction from 'the foreign gods of the land' in that the latter are partial and relative spirits whereas the God of Israel is what Krochmal calls 'absolute Spirituality', referring to Jeremiah (x, 16) for a definition : 'Not as these is the portion of Jacob, for He is the shaper of all things, and Israel is the tribe of His inheritance : the Lord of Hosts is His name.' This meant, Krochmal explained, that God is 'absolute Spirituality and there is none beside Him as the source of all spiritual being and the sum of all them that exist in themselves and their particularity i.e. in their cleaving to the hosts of heaven and to the hosts of earth, all of them finite and changing, and they do not possess the truth of existence and absolute being except insofar as they are in God, the absolute spiritual and the infinite.' Krochmal also quoted Joshua (xxii, 22): 'God of gods is the Lord.'[38]

He saw the process and purpose of the election of Israel in the decision of God

> to unite from amidst the seed [of the patriachs] by separation after separation the seed of one family, the twelve tribes of Jacob, and to establish their number as a full and distinct people in its own land in fixed borders ['He set the borders of the peoples according to the number of the children of Israel', Deuteronomy xxxii, 8] and the divine wisdom set out to direct and perfect its purpose so that it might become a kingdom of priests i.e. teachers to the human race of the absolute faith of the *Torah* . . .'[39]

Krochmal saw the contrast between Israel and the nations in terms which emphasised the primacy of intellectual insight. The Gentile peoples

> did not attain to the comprehension of the spiritual with a clarified understanding and therefore they did not reach the point of grasping that its truth and persistence are not where it exists for itself individually and attached to time and place — that in this respect it disappears and perishes — but where it is general, i.e. where it enjoys the truth of existence in the absolute spiritual and that this is a concept of the pure understanding alone . . .

That is why the worship of such peoples degenerated into abominations, their spirituality entirely died and likewise the peoples themselves. 'But through the lovingkindness of God to the people whom He chose, a lovingkindness that we cannot attach either to a cause in ourselves or in any of the generations that preceded us [i.e. until we return to our primary origins, the patriarchs, as explained in the *Torah*] there came upon us the thought supreme over all thoughts of the understanding.'[40]

This was no sudden insight. The process of understanding is protracted. If Israel chose as its God the absolute spiritual, then God also chose Israel and, furthermore, had to educate Israel to this end; for example the exodus from Canaan to Egypt was understood by Krochmal as a means to Israel's acquisition of crafts and skills, in a land, moreover, where there was no danger of their being corrupted.[41] Even the Israel which stood at Sinai did not grasp in its full purity the spiritual that was there revealed until the time of the return from Babylonian exile, about a millennium later. It was this process that equipped Israel to become 'teachers to a multitude of nations, whereby we exist to this day and with it we shall arise and be redeemed forever.'[42]

'Each spirit produces itself, i.e. its activity is its essence.'[43] Although this accounts for the eternity of Israel, through the activity of the absolute spiritual, there is no suggestion that the history of Israel is thereby removed from the realm of nature and man to that of the historically unintelligible. On the contrary, it remains subject to precisely the same laws of growth and decadence as does that of any other people.[44] But the difference, the literally vital difference, lies in the fact that the God of Israel, by virtue of its absolute quality, is also 'the guardian of Israel that does not sleep or slumber'. In the same way, as, for example, He averted assimilation to the Egyptians, so does He also ensure Israel's survival and revival, even amidst collapse. The experience of exile must therefore be irrelevant, in confirmation of which Krochmal referred to the prophet Haggai who was active in 520 BCE during the reign of Darius I, King of Persia : 'Then spoke Haggai the Lord's messenger in the Lord's message unto the people saying : "I am with you saith the Lord . . . The word that I covenanted with you when ye came out of Egypt have I established and My spirit abideth amongst you; fear ye not." '[45]

When Krochmal came to show this whole process at work in the history of Israel he introduced the notion of cycles. This was apparently its first use apart from the much earlier *Sefer Ha' Temunah* where, in any case, the nature of the cycles was very different from that postulated by Krochmal.[46] The latter's first cycle ran from the days of Abraham to the death of Gedalya b. Ahikam and was divided into three periods : (*a*) from Abraham to the Exodus from Egypt (growth); (*b*) from the conquest of Canaan to the death of Solomon (maturity and achievement); (*c*) from division of the kingdom to the death of Gedalya (decline and collapse).[47] The second cycle, which ran from the Babylonian exile to the death of Bar Kochba and the martyrdom of R. Akiba at the hands of the Romans, was introduced by Krochmal : 'despite all the defects in relation to the days of the first Temple' there grew up in the dispersed people 'a new great spirituality that waxed strong and brought to all [i.e. the exiles] a spirit of wisdom and understanding, a spirit of counsel and bravery, a spirit of knowledge and fear of the Lord.'[48] Armed in this way, Israel's second cycle passes through the three periods : (*a*) from the destruction of the Temple to the supremacy of Greece over Persia; (*b*) thenceforward to the death of Alexander Jannai and the wars amongst his sons; (*c*) from the death of Queen Alexandra to the Roman persecutions.

The two chapters in which the first two cycles are expounded (vⅢ, ⅸ) bear mottos taken respectively from Malachi and Ezekiel: 'For I the Lord change not; and ye, O Sons of Israel, are not consumed' (Malachi ⅲ, 6); 'And I will put My spirit in you, and ye shall live, and I shall place you in your own land' (Ezekiel xxxvⅡ, 14). The third cycle does not receive the same attention, but the first period (of growth) can be said to stretch from the Antonines to the beginning of the Gaonic period, with the people 'plucked like a brand from the fire'; the second, thenceforward to the Golden Age of Spanish Jewry; and the third, from the death of Maimonides and Nahmanides to the period of expulsion and the Khmelnitzky pogroms in Poland (1648–9).[49]

This is the process that Krochmal, after referring to 'the melting and disintegration' of the other peoples, describes as follows :

> such is the case in which the spiritual is particular and therefore finite and fated to collapse. But in our people, although in relation to materiality and sensuous externality, we too are subordinated to the laws of nature already mentioned, despite this the situation is in accordance with the words of our sages : 'exiled to Elam, the Divine Presence was with them etc.' (T. B. *Megillah* 29a) i.e. the universal spiritual in our midst will protect us and save us from the law of all those subject to change. And all that is easily deduced from what is said above. Thus we have seen fit to recall the periods that have passed over us from the time of the growth of the people until today, in order to show how the periods of the three cycles which we have mentioned were duplicated and triplicated in us and how, when the days of disintegration and destruction were fulfilled, there was always renewed in us a new spirit and new life; and if we

fell, how we arose and were encouraged and the Lord our God did not abandon us.[50]

It is not clear whether a fourth cycle has begun or whether an entirely new phase of Israel's existence has opened since the mid-seventeenth century.[51]

If this description of the unique, undying and all-encompassing spirituality of Israel is juxtaposed to the other argument that, as Krochmal put it for example early in his chapter on Hegel, 'it is one of the principles of the religio-Biblical belief that the whole human race will return in unison in the knowledge of God, but only in the end of days',[52] then his understanding of the centrality of Israel can be grasped. It is to the Oneness embodied in Israel that the lesser and transient spirits of the peoples will return, thus making Israel the centre of the world. It seems clear that Krochmal grasped the course of world history as the union of the scattered spirits of the peoples with the primal spirituality of which they have always been a separated part.

Now and again, Graetz also resounded with a touch of Krochmal. Impressed, for example, by the recuperative phenomenon of Jewish history – 'a brand snatched from the fire' – Graetz like his predecessor argued that the history of Israel 'does not merely show as in the case of other peoples the alternation of growth, efflorescence and decay, but also the extraordinary phenomenon that decay was again followed by a new growth and a new blossoming and that this rise and fall is repeated three times.'[53] Overwhelmingly, however, Graetz's conception of the 'idea of Judaism' and therefore of the course of Jewish history is vastly different from that of Krochmal. Graetz knew nothing of the 'lesser spirits' of other peoples; nor did he know of any cyclical movement in the activity of spirit. His theory had none of the biologico-organic character of Krochmal's and was to this extent more abstract and intellectualistic and more simple. But it was also more concrete in that Graetz rationalised his understanding of Israel's history as a messianic progress towards embodiment in an actual reality.

This was the achievement of Graetz's early essay of 1846 (repr. Berlin, 1936), 'Die Konstruktion der jüdischen Geschichte'. The essay opened with the question : 'What is Judaism?' The elucidation of this, the idea, would *eo ipso* provide the elucidation to the movement of the historical world. Judaism became manifest through its history in so comprehensive a manner as to validate all the diverse definitions of Judaism, which 'are all true if they are understood as separate factors [*Momente*] in the absolute basic principle of Judaism. But they are all false if they wish to be understood as basic . . . the totality of Judaism is only recognisable through its history; in history its whole essence, the sum of its powers must be made explicit.'[54] There was even in the apparent vagaries of the haphazard a uniform idea, and Graetz compared history to 'nothing but the buds of the idea, and the manifoldness of forms in which history delights are nothing more than the *Momente* of the idea which have become concrete.'[55]

The idea is spirit and transcendence as against the immanent paganism of nature, borne out by extension in the idol-worship, nature-worship and the plastic art of pagans such as the Greeks.[56] This idea of the spirit of the divine does not exist for its own sake – it exists in order to be incorporated in a state : '*die Gottesidee soll zugleich Staatsidee sein*'. There are laws, 'so that it may go well with you'. Judaism is a state law (*Staatsgesetz*). It has a social and political no less than a dogmatic and religious aspect, the concrete expression of which is 'the revealed Law – the *Torah* – and the Holy Land – the Law is the soul, the Holy Land the body, of this unique state-organism.' The land exists as a precise area 'for the unhindered unfolding of the laws which characterise the God-idea in its fullness and the Law in turn exists in order to further the social well-being of Israel. The *Torah*, the Israelite nation and the Holy Land stand, I might say, in a magical rapport.' Graetz compared a Judaism that lacked 'the firm soil of state life' to 'a hollowed-out half-uprooted tree'.[57] Judiasm is therefore no religion of the present but of the future. Its patriarchs lived in promises and in their present saw 'only a preparation for the future of their progeny'. Judaism, likewise, 'struggles for a present that it lacks'. It lives between the memory of Sinai and the anticipation of the *Zeitenideal* of the prophets.

At this level of abstraction Graetz saw a two-fold division in the idea, and consequently in the history, of Judaism : in its pre-exilic phase it bore a predominantly political character; in its post-exilic phase predominantly a religious character. But in both periods, Graetz wrote, 'Judaism knows itself to be one and the same, it bears within itself this self-consciousness, that with all the

variety of external experience and inner metamorphoses it constitutes for itself an indissoluble unity.'[58] But this oneness will only
be made real in the course of history.

These preliminary words of Graetz delineated the standard, the
model, the ideal, by which he assessed the empirical reality of
Jewish history. To this assessment he devoted the remainder of the
Konstruktion: not by way of cycles or the dialectic negation of one
stage of the idea of Judaism by its successor, but with the *unilinear*
unfolding, as Graetz puts it, of 'the tree [already contained] in the
seed'.[59] The idea of Judaism remains an unchanging entity, only
externally involved in the world's history. Essentially it remained
apart, unfolding changes in form, however, which Graetz now
identified. He expounded three periods in this unfolding, each
divided in three phases, with frequent analogies and parallels
amongst them. The first period began with the Israelites' crossing
of the Jordan under Joshua (earlier events are not mentioned by
Graetz and do not appear to enjoy normal historical status) and
came to an end with the Babylonian exile.[60] The politico-social
factor was generally predominant but Graetz traced its gradual
evolution into the religious. He identified three phases : the dissolution of the tribal system, rectified in part by the Judges; the
emerging presence of the religious factor with the prophet Samuel,
last of the Judges, which movement was later enhanced by the
centralisation of worship at the Temple; and the further decline
of the political factor with the division of the kingdom, which by
the same token brought the religious to prominence and culminated in the exile of the ten tribes and the collapse of Israel. The
prophets formed the bond between the conclusion of the first
and the beginning of the second period (though they by no means
limited their concern to religious matters, but included foreign
and political affairs; for example, Isaiah cautioned against sub-
ordination to Assyria, and Jeremiah urged submission to Chal-
daean power).[61]

At this point Judaism entered into its second period. 'If, in the
first period, the political factor [*das Staatliche*] stood out with
exclusive one-sidedness, then the second period drove the religious
factor into a one-sided position, to the extent that it negated all
political independence; Judaism ceased to be a basic state law
and became religion in the accepted sense of the word.'[62] This
period lasted until the destruction of the state, the Second Temple

and the beginnings of the Diaspora. In its first phase the religious factor, weak as yet, strove for 'consolidation', and this led Graetz, in the first of numerous inter-period analogies, to echo the Talmudic comparison of Moses and Ezra, and, furthermore, to see a parallel between the Judges and the Men of the Great Assembly (though the former had to contend with political and the latter with religious anarchy).[63] With the growth of this phase the religious factor created for itself 'a central point and a corpus of bearers [Trägerschaft]'. These arose through reaction against the incursion of victorious hellenism in the wake of Alexander the Great's campaigns. Characteristic of this phase were the Maccabees, with Johanan Hyrkanos the parallel to David, though again the adjustment must be made between the religious wars of the former, and the political wars of the latter. In the third phase of this period Graetz saw another parallel between the division of Israel/Judah and the division of the Pharisees/Sadducees, though again, in keeping with the overall evolution of the idea of Judaism, the transposition must be made from politics to religion. He also compared the prophetic schools to the enlarged Sanhedrin as focuses of religious interest.[64]

Graetz termed the third period the Diaspora. It differed fundamentally from its predecessors in that the religious factor reached its culminating point 'in unreflecting immediacy ... it took a completely external artless course'. Now in the third and final period of the Diaspora, the religious factor 'sinks itself in the inwardness of reflection, it seeks the knowledge of its own being and its meaning'. Whereas the idea of Judaism had hitherto been externally involved in all the workings and conflicts of world history, 'it now withdraws into itself, it seeks to comprehend itself consciously, it seeks to assure itself of its content, it seeks to be explained through mediation and theory.' In accordance with this change, the sages, sectarians and the righteous of the previous period gave way to scholars, thinkers, philosophers of religion, systematicians – 'even sceptics and apostates', said Graetz, 'for scepticism is a necessary ingredient in the purificatory process of knowing.' Self-conscious thinking took grip of 'all the data of [Judaism's] earlier historical life'.[65] This reflective tendency marked the first phase of the new period. It was characterised by allegory, mysticism and *aggada*. The work of Saadya Gaon (882–942) marked the turning point to the second phase in that he was the last to compose a commentary on the Pentateuch full of philosophical reflections but was also the first commentator able to make these reflections into a system. Maimonides continued and completed this line of development and in the subsequent controversy over the 'Guide', Graetz saw a reinforcement of the theoretical definition of Judaism, if not in intensity, then at least in extension.[66] The third period differed fundamentally from its two predecessors in that it had nothing new to add to the essential idea of Judaism. What it does contribute is the factor of self-consciousness; this is the period when Judaism became conscious of itself, reflected on its two earlier manifestations, and concluded therefrom that its task was to bring into being what Graetz called 'a religious state-constitution', earlier defined as a practice in accordance with theory, a religio-social reality.[67] Graetz identified the opening of the third phase with the work of Moses Mendelssohn and soon saw with confidence that 'a good beginning had been made in bringing to consciousness the different sides of Judaism in their fullness and wealth of content.' He found this embodied in the manner in which Steinheim had enunciated the metaphysical, S. R. Hirsch the religious, and Joseph Salvador the socio-legislative aspect of Judaism.[68] This prefigured the comprehensive principle that would unite all viewpoints and be reflected in all manifestations of Jewish life.

When Krochmal had reached this point he had recourse to an image and evoked the union of the scattered, transient spirits of the peoples with the undying oneness of the God or Spirit of Israel. Graetz, on the other hand, sought to express this notion in empirical terms.

In the *Konstruktion* for example, Graetz already associated himself with the prophetic assurance that the *judentümliche Gottesidee* would not remain limited to Israel 'but would extend to the whole of mankind'.[69] This subdued reference to the notion of a Jewish 'mission' to spread the truths of Judaism – if indeed this is what Graetz meant at all in 1846 – was far surpassed in certain essays he published in the latter half of his career. In so doing he came close to the missionary ideal of that Reform Judaism which was otherwise repugnant to him.[70] Basing himself on the prophecies of Deutero-Isaiah, Graetz saw Israel as the 'Messiah-people'. Whereas most of the prophets attributed messianic majesty to the descendants of David, in the eyes of Deutero-

Isaiah this concept disappeared, 'in the presence of the ideal greatness of all Israel'. The figure of the suffering servant, 'precisely because of its suffering' is called to great things. No other prophet, Graetz declared, had so clearly proclaimed the universality of Judaism in its mission to convert enemies into friends. He quoted LVI, 6–7 : 'Also the aliens, that join themselves to the Lord, to minister unto Him, And to love the name of the Lord, To be His servants, Every one that keepeth the Sabbath from profaning it, And holdeth fast by My covenant : Even them will I bring to My holy mountain, and make them joyful in My house of prayer . . . For My house shall be called a house of prayer for all peoples.'[71]

Graetz derived this promise from the fact that 'the Israelite tribe has for centuries proven itself powerful and productive in religious and moral truths for the salvation of mankind.' It has, 'so to speak, an innate disposition' for religious creativity that showed no diminution from Moses to the present day.'[72] The special faculty of the Jews to serve as 'a light unto the nations', as a 'Messiah-people', Graetz attributed to their inherent moral superiority over contemporary European civilisation. The latter he saw corrupted by the spread of venereal disease, prostitution, illegitimacy, and the cult of Aphrodite and Mary Magdalene in the art galleries of Europe. He contrasted the chastity and abstemiousness of the Jews, whose sexual hygiene was the key to their survival and health, with the corruption of their neighbours.[73]

In this 'missionary' phase, which culminated in the last years of Graetz's life, he did not by any means renounce the unity of land, people and *Torah* but in the exile of the Jews he did see a beneficent providence at work. He made of the Diaspora 'a blessing in the development of the world's history'. Israel's very wanderings enabled it 'to fulfil its mission to bring light to the nations'. From the 'sparks' that Israel scattered at Alexandria, Antioch and Rome there came the birth of Christianity. The 'seeds' that Israel scattered in Mecca and Medina gave rise to Islam. 'From a few traces of light left by it was derived scholastic philosophy in the second half of the Middle Ages, and the Protestantism of the Continent in the sixteenth century . . .'[74]

By comparison with this schema, Krochmal did not succeed in making Israel's history the empirical exemplar of his theory. Despite, or perhaps because of, this attempt to encompass the totality of Jewish history, Krochmal did not resolve the tension or duality between the religio-metaphysical elements in his teaching and the human. Growth, decay, etc. are the result of natural and human factors but their nullification is the work of the 'absolute spiritual'. Their interaction is not shown at work. It seems that Krochmal engaged himself in what was certainly an unsuccessful endeavour to unite the historical and the non-historical.

But a far more interesting question concerns the relationship amongst the cycles. Do they repeat each other or does each represent progress over its predecessor? There is certainly no antithetical or dialectical relationship amongst them. The biologico-organic system of Krochmal rules this out of court. On *a priori* grounds alone, however, each rebirth must inherit at least some spiritual enrichment from its predecessor(s) and not constitute a start *de novo*. To suppose otherwise would be to deny the rationality of the absolute Spiritual. Krochmal himself pointed out that the revelation at Sinai was not understood 'in the purity of its truth' until a millenium had passed, with the return of the exiles from Babylon.[75] It does in fact, seem clear that the cycles do show progress over each other, especially the second over the first.[76]

But is the further conclusion justified that the cyclical period might come to an end altogether, yielding to some consummation of history? No clarity emerges. True, Krochmal nowhere explicitly mentions a fourth cycle following the three he has already delineated; true, at least once he also refers to 'the depth of the end of days, the time in which we live' – a term, in the words of one interpreter, 'with unmistakably eschatalogical undertones'.[77] But no conclusion can safely be made *ex silentio* or on the basis of a scattered phrase. It seems safe, on the other hand, to argue that the relationship between the cycles and the progress that each represents over its predecessor is to be evaluated in terms of the increased spiritual insight that each cycle brings with it. This means that at the time Krochmal was writing – in the first half of the nineteenth century – the fourth cycle is unfolding a reflective knowledge of Judaism which is thereby becoming more and more conscious of itself and its past.[78]

If this is so, then at this level the analyses of Graetz and Krochmal coincide. The *Geschichte* itself suggests that now (i.e. the mid-eighteenth century onwards) Judaism is entering a period of 'growing self-consciousness'.[79] In the *Konstruktion* likewise, Graetz suggests that in the mid-nineteenth century 'the different sides of Judaism' are being raised to the conscious level in the work of Steinheim (the metaphysical), S. R. Hirsch (the religious) and Joseph Salvador (the socio-legislative).[80] This is a fruit of self-reflection from which it would presumably follow that this achievement at the level of the idea of Judaism would be accompanied by the realisation of the idea. Is not history 'the reflection of the idea'?[81] Again, if this is so, then Krochmal and Graetz must agree that if the idea of Judaism has become fully self-conscious of itself, then the condition for a messianic consummation has been fulfilled.

D

7 The Apotheosis of History: Dubnow

History becomes a surrogate for Judaism in the work of Dubnow, at the end of the nineteenth century. Dubnow was born in 1860 in Mstislav (Mohilev, White Russia). At one level he can be regarded as a Jewish parallel to those other contemporary historians of central and eastern Europe who made historical consciousness the bearer and, to some extent, the awakener of national identity (e.g. Palacky – Bohemia; Lipinsky – Ukraine; Lelewel – Poland). Dubnow too made the study of Jewish history, with the concomitant development of Jewish historical consciousness, a principal bearer of Jewish existence. At a deeper level Dubnow's outlook epitomises that situation in which nothing remains to the Jew save his history. That is all he has left. A knowledge of history, Dubnow held, has to replace, was in fact already replacing, the authorities and sanctions of the past. In the days of antiquity what he called 'the triple agencies' of the state, race and religion had formed Israel into a single nation. During its dispersion these had been chiefly replaced by religious consciousness. But 'in our days', marked by the leaven of liberal ideas, marked also by 'abrupt differences' in regard to faith and cult, when 'traditional Judaism . . . is proving powerless to hold together the diverse factors of the national organism – in these days the keystone of national unity seems to be the historical consciousness.' He repeats : 'upon the knowledge of history, then, depends the strength of the national consciousness'.[1] That is why, when Dubnow summoned Russian Jewry in 1892 to seek out and assemble all the neglected archival material relating to its past, he termed this activity 'a national matter'.[2] In Russia, as in Germany a century earlier, it was natural that the historical impetus should emanate from the alienated circles of the Jewish enlightenment.[3]

Dubnow's early experiences predisposed him in this direction. He was a *révolté* against the traditional Talmudic culture of his environment and struggled towards an outlook that was unhesitatingly secular. In challenging his environment Dubnow drew support from the philosophic liberalism and the individualism of John Stuart Mill:

> the problem that he [Mill] encountered in respect of the freedom of the individual, the liberation of the soul of the individual from the dominance of the public or the tyranny of public opinion was close to my heart because of my own bitter experience. Was I not myself a victim of this tyranny which entitled my parents to give me an education accepted in its time . . . and were not my wanderings and restlessness to a large extent caused by the fact that with my ideas of freedom I could not live amongst the religious zealots of my native town. And now appeared the great thinker, one of the greatest of his generation, and proved irrefutably that it is not enough to fight for the political freedom of the collective against the tyranny of the ruling minority but that there is also a need to wage war for the freedom of the individual against the tyranny of the majority, against prevailing tradition and accepted views.[4]

For many years pictures of Mill and Shelley stood on Dubnow's work-table.

Dubnow developed an outlook that was uncompromisingly secular. He argued, for example, not that God created man in his image, but that 'the people created God in *its* image. This was a historical god who directed the historical destinies of the people but was at the same time their product.'[5] Similarly, he saw in the Talmud a means to self-preservation, an expression of ultra-nationalism, an intellectual exercise and a compendium of casuistry.[6]

These views can be related to a particular period in the history of the Jewish enlightenment, the *Haskalah*, and the Russian intelligentsia. A determining influence on Dubnow's outlook came from his reading of English and French thinkers, as distinct from German thinkers who had earlier been dominant in the *Haskalah*. At the same time Dubnow can also been seen in the context of the Russian social thought that developed in the nineteenth century. In this perspective we can perhaps see in Dubnow a curious blend of Westerner and Judeophile. Dubnow, as heir to the *Haskalah*, not only welcomed the secularisation of Jewish life (though with a difference) but also incorporated in his work much of the outlook and values of the Russian intelligentsia of the nineteenth century. He was no Bazarov or Pisarev in their denial of spirituality, but the cast of his mind was undoubtedly secular, rationalist and utilitarian in the spirit of the men of the 1860s and 1870s. In adolescence, when Dubnow rejected the traditionalist Jewish values of his early background and upbringing, the materialism of Tchernishevsky and Dobrolyubov or the populism of Mikhailovsky became important forces in the formation of his outlook.[7]

Moreover, Russian was in a sense Dubnow's mother tongue. He wrote all his major works in Russian – save his *History of Hassidism* (Hebrew) – spoke Russian at home with his family, wrote his autobiography in Russian, generally used Russian for his public declarations and, in fact, spent much of his life until 1918 in such Russian cultural centres as Odessa and St Petersburg. He lived physically remote from the Yiddish-speaking centres of the Pale (though not without exalting Hebrew and Yiddish as national languages).[8]

In socio-political terms Dubnow was further related to his time in that he also shared in the nationalist strivings of the peoples of the multi-national empires of eastern and central Europe. His national emphasis on the Jews as makers of history and not merely as a people that subjectively experienced a history imposed on them by others, has an obvious affiliation with the assertion of the rights of small nations in the second half of the nineteenth century: '. . . the course of history is directed, not toward the subjection of national groups but toward their liberation', he wrote in 1901. 'If the nineteenth century was able to secure the legal recognition by the community of the principle of freedom of the individual, the twentieth century is faced with the task of establishing the freedom or the autonomy of the national individual . . . Israel is not alone in this struggle.'[9] This clearly flowed from Dubnow's perception of the position of the Jews in the contemporary Tsarist Empire where, it has been established, more than 95 per cent of the Jews lived amongst other minority peoples – Poles, White Russians, Ukrainians, Lithuanians, etc.[10]

In this continuing phenomenon of Jewish identity Dubnow saw a prefiguring of the movement of those national minorities who sought some form of independent existence within the multi-national empires of their day. He made the customary distinction between nationality and state, and welcomed, as confirmation of his own views, the theories that the Austrian Social-Democrat, Springer, put forward in 'Der Kampf der oesterreichischen Nationen um den Staat' (Leipzig, Vienna, 1902). Dubnow appreciated Springer's argument that the person, rather than the territory, be the criterion for the form of autonomous government of a minority group – 'an Austrian and a Jewish autonomist arrive at the same conclusion regarding the problem of the national community and the type of unit for self-determination . . .'[11]

He defined a nation as 'an historico-cultural group which is conscious of itself as a nation even though it may have lost all or some of the external characteristics of nationality (state, territory, language) provided it possesses the determination to continue developing its own personality in the future. Objective criteria of nationality are giving way . . . to subjective factors.' The references here are to Fichte (though with reservations), Renan, Fouillée, and Rudolph Springer (Karl Renner).[12] But it remained objective to the extent that Dubnow also believed that 'a person is not made a member of this nationality or that, but is born into it . . . it is impossible for a person "to be made" a member of a natural collective group, of a tribe, or people, except through mingling of blood (through marriage) in the course of generations, through the prolonged process of shedding one's national individuality.'[13] This remained a national–secular conception of nationhood. Dubnow deplored in Judaism the mutual interpenetration of national and religious categories so that a Spinoza, for example, was, on religious grounds, forced to withdraw from the Jewish community. Had the criterion of membership been purely national, no such loss would have been necessary.[14] Again a qualification is necessary : although Dubnow argued that to be a Jew one must be born a Jew, and, that this did not necessarily require any specific religious commitment to Judaism, he also maintained that conversion to another faith did remove a Jew from the nation, for 'under conditions prevailing in the Diaspora' conversion meant separation from the Jewish nation, that is to say 'exit from Judaism by acceptance of the Christian religion means exit from the Jewish nation'.[15]

All this national and secular emphasis did set Dubnow apart from Graetz. But towards the beginning of Dubnow's career this was not immediately apparent. He did himself have some initial sympathy with Graetz and see the diaspora history of Israel in the light of the familiar distinction between the predominantly intellectual and the spiritual history of the Jews – 'to think and to suffer' – and the material and national history of the world in general. The former

> has no diplomatic artifices, no wars, no campaigns, no un-warranted encroachments backed by armed force upon the rights of other nations, nothing of all that constitutes the chief content – the monotonous and for the most part idea-less content – of many other chapters in the history of the world . . . Before our eyes passes a long procession of facts from the fields of intellectual effort, of morality, religion, and social converse. Finally, the thrilling drama of Jewish martyrdom is unrolled to our astonished gaze. If the inner life and the social and intellectual development of a people form the kernel of history, and politics and occasional wars are but its husk, then certainly the history of the Jewish diaspora is all kernel.[16]

But in his maturity Dubnow moved towards a more 'material' conception of Jewish history. Graetz, the admirers of Dubnow have argued, 'was so deeply bound up (*versponnen*) in the inner history of Judaism that he almost completely overlooked the continuity of its external history.'[17] It has correspondingly been claimed that Dubnow overcame Graetz's deficiency by substituting a 'sociological' for an 'ideological conception' of Jewish history.[18] Certainly, one theme of paramount importance in the fifty-odd years between the publication of Graetz's last volume (1876) and Dubnow's first (1925) was the attempt to overcome Graetz's neglect of daily life and the material life of the individual.[19]

Dubnow himself complained that Graetz had unduly limited the subject-matter of his history of the Diaspora to the intellectual and the martyrological.[20] His own aspirations were in marked contrast. Dubnow aimed to create what he called a sociological history, and this he differentiated sharply from the 'one-sided conception of "post-Bibilical" history' à la Zunz and Graetz, divided into Talmudic, gaonic, rabbinic, mystical and enlightenment periods. These might be appropriate to a literary history but in no wise to a national history.[21]

Dubnow's encounter with Comte was of crucial importance to his historical understanding. He described Comte's theory of the three stages of thought as a 'revelation'. To put sociology, as did Comte, at the summit of the sciences, seemed to Dubnow 'the highest truth'. Further suspicion of metaphysics came to Dubnow from his reading of Feuerbach and Büchner.[22] He then assimilated Comte's theory according to his own historiographical requirements. Dubnow distinguished three consecutive stages in the evolution of the understanding of Jewish history : first, the *theological* understanding of the Bible; second, the *spiritual* understanding of a Zunz or a Graetz which denied to the Jews, through their lack of territory and state, an active share in the determination of their own history but condemned them to be the passive object of the history of other peoples (these historians must accordingly attune their periodisation to the history of literature and culture); third, the attainment in modern times of a *sociological* conception. To Dubnow this was a 'purely scientific conception' and based itself on the view that

the Jewish people has at all times and in all countries, always and everywhere, been the subject, the creator of its own history, not only in the intellectual sphere but also in the general sphere of social life. During the period of its political independence as well as in its stateless period, Judaism stands among the other nations, not merely as a religious community, but with the distinctive characteristics of a nation . . . [which] fought always and everywhere for its autonomous existence in the sphere of social life as well as in all other spheres of cultural activity.[23]

Armed with this sociological conception, which comprehended Jewish history as the history of a society that was at the same time a nation, Dubnow articulated an exposition of that society's history as a succession of changing autonomous centres – Babylon, Spain, Germany, Poland–Lithuania. In his own day, Dubnow hoped to see the *Synagogengemeinden* or *Cultusgemeinden* of Germany overcome their limitations as religious bodies and become *Volksgemeinden*, i.e. secular national autonomous communities. In eastern Europe, where the Jews did not even enjoy citizen rights, this must remain a hope for the future. But since he was also writing during the era of the mass migration of Jews from eastern Europe to the western world, especially the United States, Dubnow argued that there, where the government was neither authoritarian nor concerned with the private lives of its citizens, 'Jews could enjoy even now a large measure of self-administration if only they were willing to advance beyond the confines of the "religious community" . . .'[24]

There was already in Graetz some suggestion of Jewish history as composed of a succession of changing centres; for example, he saw Babylon, the seat of the Gaonate, 'as the unifying centre-point of the widespread Jewish diaspora'. Even before this collapsed, a 'new centre of gravity' was formed in Spain. In southern France and in Lorraine further 'foci' arose.[25] But Dubnow used the notion of 'changing centres' as the very articulation of his idea of Jewish history : most of all so, because such centres were the organ of Jewish self-government.

As distinct from Graetz, Dubnow organised his material in terms of these changing hegemonic centres. After the collapse of the Jewish state he began with the hegemony of Palestine under the rule of pagan Rome (first to fourth centuries of the Christian era). He followed this with the hegemony of Palestine and Babylon under the rule of Christian Rome, Byzantium and Persia (fourth to seventh centuries); then Babylonian hegemony at the time of the Arabian Khalifate up to the collapse of the oriental centres of Jewish life (seventh to eleventh centuries). Dubnow turned now from the East to Europe and in succession to the Jewish centres in Arabic Spain (ninth to twelfth centuries) : the Franco-Spanish hegemony (thirteenth century); the Spanish–German hegemony (fourteenth to fifteenth centuries); the hegemony of the Ashkenazim, especially in the blossoming of the Jewish autonomous centre in Poland (sixteenth to seventeenth centuries). There followed a period of transition, and then the concept of national or quasi-national centres gave way, from the French Revolution onwards, to a Europe-wide treatment conceived mainly in terms of the struggle for emancipation. It followed from this that the Diaspora was not an anomaly, as the Zionists claimed, but, as Dubnow argued in the article on the Diaspora that he contributed to the *Encyclopaedia of the Social Sciences*, the scene of 'substitutes for state forms', i.e. autonomous communities controlling not only religious life but also social relations, with their own educational and charitable institutions and enjoying in some cases power of taxation and judicial administration. This is what Dubnow meant when he wrote to his English translator, Isaiah Friedländer, in December 1913 : 'I occupied myself with the history of the people, not with the history of literature, and history is essentially the development or decline of the national self in relation to the environment.'[26]

It was in the institution of the Council of the Four Lands (Greater Poland, Lesser Poland, Lvov, Volhynia) from the sixteenth to the eighteenth centuries that Dubnow saw the paramount embodiment of his ideal, both as historian and Jewish nationalist. In his introduction to the *Pinkas* (Record Book) of the Council governing Lithuanian Jewry he proclaimed that this Council was 'one link in the chain of autonomy – the independent rule of the communities of Israel in all lands. If it were not for this chain which links all the scattered Diaspora, Israel could not have existed in the generations following the destruction of its kingdom and its land.' He transformed into a positive virtue the reproach that the Jews constituted 'a state within a state' : 'Yes, a state within a state, an internally autonomous collective within an external political group, and thus the nature of things requires.' He drew authority from Genesis xxxxix, 10 : 'The sceptre shall not depart from Judah'. He furthermore proclaimed that this was the path of the future – 'and the new movement of the "national minorities" in the states of Europe proves it'. Dubnow saw an overriding connection between the Sanhedrin in Yavneh, the Gaonate in Babylon, the *aljama* in Spain, the rabbinical assemblies in France and Germany, and the Councils of Poland and Lithuania.[27]

These institutions represented to Dubnow the proof of Israel's unique destiny thus far. What may be termed Dubnow's theory of 'the chosen people' grew out of this situation. He argued that Jewish history displayed unprecedented qualities of survival to an extent that entitled the Jews to regard themselves as the bearers of a unique destiny, expressed in socio-historical terms. Dubnow, unlike Graetz, certainly did not hold that there was an unchanging idea embodied in Judaism. On the contrary, he declared himself a Spencerian evolutionist and he summoned to his aid the Russian populist, Lavrov, to deny any such proposition.[28] Rather, Dubnow perceived in the course of Jewish history a purposeful threefold development which he expressly related to the theories expounded by Alfred Fouillée in his *Esquisse psychologique des peuples européens* (1903). A national type evolves from 'the material to the spiritual and from external simplicity to inner complexity'. Initially, the nation took shape as a mere product of nature, a racial or tribal group, formed by a common origin, territory and climate which, in their turn, determined the physical and mental characteristics of the tribe (for example the wanderings of the semitic groups in Mesopotamia, Palestine, Egypt). In time, as a result of economic co-operation and other forms of human association, a further degree of organisation was reached, i.e. a civic union or state. The tribe's territory, hitherto merely part of the natural environment, became an active political factor uniting one or more tribes into a nation, with an organised political authority to determine laws, defend frontiers, assert the nation's rights and so on. At this point what Dubnow termed the 'territorial-political type of nationality' emerged (e.g. political unification under the first kings – Saul, David, Solomon). It was marked by the growth of spiritual creativity, by the elevation of religion to 'a comprehensive world view', by a deepening of the moral sense. The testing time of the maturity of such a territorial-political nation was reached, however, when it lost not only its political independence, but also its territory: 'if . . . such a nation still maintains itself for many years, creates an independent existence, reveals a stubborn determination to carry on its autonomous development – such a people has reached the highest stage of cultural-historical individuality . . .' History has chosen for this unique status the people of Israel: 'The spiritual elements outweighed decisively the material and political elements'.[29] Israel is thus the most historical of all peoples, because it has not only made its mark on human history but has also lived through all stages of human history thus far. Dubnow drove the argument home with a quotation from Pascal (*Pensées*, ii, 7) prefixed to his essay on the philosophy of Jewish history: 'Le peuple juif n'est seulement considérable par son antiquité, mais il est encore singulier en sa durée, qui a toujours continué depuis son origine jusqu'à maintenant . . . S'étendant depuis les premiers temps jusqu'aux derniers, l'histoire des juifs enferme dans sa durée celle de toutes les histoires.'

The thesis of Israel as the uniquely historical nation informed Dubnow's historiography in general. In contradistinction to Zionism, for example, which was 'principally based on the experiences of the nineteenth century', Dubnow argued that his theory of 'spiritual nationalism' was derived from 'the whole course of Jewish history'.[30]

Thus, whatever Springer and the Austro-Marxists might propose as a future socio-political arrangement, they were, in fact, merely following in the footsteps of Israel. Not only was Israel not alone in its present endeavours but it had in fact preceded all other nations along the path to autonomy.

In treating of the Jews sociologically and in terms of a national entity, Dubnow not only made them a nation apart, at a higher level of historical development, but also filled the neutral categories of historico-sociological enquiry with a theme drawn from the messianic past. He had no use for Krochmal's 'metaphysics' or for Graetz's 'spiritual' historiography – and in any case Dubnow's avowedly secular approach must inhibit his use of religious motifs. It is also true that Dubnow's whole political and social outlook, given its indebtedness to Comte, Herbert Spencer, Mill and the ideology of nineteenth-century European nationalism, was powerfully influenced by the theory of progress. Even so, with all these qualifications, the messianic category is not inappropriate. Dubnow must of course exclude any notion of Israel's restoration to the Promised Land. Also, of course, there is no suggestion here of any precipitate breakthrough to a new world. What there is, however, is the uniqueness of Israel, as proven not only in the mark it has made on human history but also in its ability to pass through all the known stages of human history : it has been a tribe; it has had a state; it has lost its state and become a spiritual nation. Of course, such an evolution is, in principle, open to any tribe. There is nothing inherently unique to Israel that has given it this ability. But the fact remains that hitherto only Israel has made this journey, to become the veritable embodiment of history. But this is not by any means a deification of survival *tel quel*. Dubnow's version of the traditional religious notion of the 'eternity of Israel' is also accompanied by the claim that purposive survival has brought Israel to a status of superiority. It has become detached from all earthly trammels to live an existence derived from subjective spiritual factors alone; and, moreover, there is here a model for all other nations or peoples. Israel has pioneered a style of life that is an exemplar. 'From Zion goes forth the Law' – and it is a law of historical evolution. Dubnow abstracted from the elements of prophetic messianism sufficient to inform his own model of historical evolution.

It is this, however, that also produced the division in his outlook between the course of history (as regards Israel) and the political imperatives he drew from it. If the highest stage of history is that of 'spiritual nationhood' – open in principle to any nation – it is odd and even contradictory that Dubnow should seek a (lower) territorial framework of existence as a setting for Jewish life – i.e. in some sort regress from subjectivity to objectivity, through the institutionalisation of communal self-government on a territorial basis.

An equally telling objection came from Ahad Ha'Am, no less an admirer of Mill and Spencer and liberal values than Dubnow himself.[31] But he assailed Dubnow for his advocacy of Yiddish, accusing him of attempting to create 'new literary and cultural values which will be a sort of imitation, a reflection of a reflection, of foreign cultures, on the model of the Lithuanians and the Ruthenes, adding 'I can see no reason and no need in such a lowly national existence'.[32] This criticism is made on the narrow 'Yiddish' front, of course. But it has a wider application, for the sort of national existence that Dubnow ascribed to the destiny of Israel, however unique, lacked a purpose. It would seem indeed that Israel had already achieved its end, demonstrating to the full its ability to lead an unattached national existence. Could it therefore have any further to go?

8 History Denied: Rosenzweig

History conceived as the history of the rabbinic *Kabbalah* did not survive the eighteenth century; history conceived as the identification of the messiah flourished, with all its protean changes of form, into the twentieth century. But the work of Franz Rosenzweig made a consistent attempt to identify Judaism, not with history, but with meta-history. Where previous Jewish thinkers sought for the messiah in and through the movement of history, to Rosenzweig this was a forlorn endeavour. The messiah, admittedly, had not come; yet the Jew already lived in the kingdom of heaven.

From Rosenzweig came the counter to Dubnow and to all who sought to understand Judaism historically. Rosenzweig and Dubnow did indeed have something in common, for example a negative outlook on Zionism and a corresponding acceptance of the Diaspora.[1] But their reasons were in each case different. If Dubnow saw Israel as the historical people *par excellence*, for it had lived through all phases of human history thus far, Rosenzweig utterly denied that the category of history could at all contribute to the understanding of Israel. There was not even a conventional sense in which Israel could be said to have a history. He could never say with Graetz, for example, 'that the totality of Judaism is only visible through its history'.[2] With equal emphasis must Rosenzweig reject the notion of a divinely governed Jewish history, as enunciated by Krochmal. In a diary entry dating from his early twenties, Rosenzweig refused to see God in history. 'We see God in each ethical action, but not in the finished whole, in history; for why would we need a God, if history were divine?' In an explicit confrontation with Hegel, Rosenzweig argued that 'the only true theodicy' is religion. 'The struggle against history in the nineteenth-century sense is therefore for us simultaneously the struggle for religion in the twentieth-century sense.'[3]

Rosenzweig was born to assimilated middle-class parents in Cassel in 1886.[4] A most important part of his early education at various German universities (Göttingen, Munich, Leipzig, Berlin) was the period of four years, 1908–12, that he devoted to the study of history under Friedrich Meinecke at Freiburg. A late fruit of this study was Rosenzweig's doctoral thesis *Hegel und der Staat* (2 vols, Munich, Berlin, 1920), inspired and influenced by the chapter on Hegel in Meinecke's *Weltbürgertum und Nationalstaat* (1908). The work also bore the influence of Dilthey.[5] Meinecke offered his pupil an academic post at Freiburg but Rosenzweig declined in favour of his overriding commitment to study and teaching in the Jewish field. In 1920 he was appointed head of the Freies Jüdisches Lehrhaus in Frankfurt a.M., and only a year later the first edition of *Der Stern der Erlösung* appeared. It had originated in 1918 in the postcards sent home by Unteroffizier Rosenzweig, then serving on the Balkan front with a German anti-aircraft unit. Here, and in his other writings, until his death in 1929, Rosenzweig elaborated an understanding of Jewish meta-historical existence.

But of course he did this in the context of his own time. Rosenzweig had first to overcome the influence of the idealism of Hegel and Fichte and their Jewish analogue or counterpart: religious liberalism as embodied for example, in the idea of progress, or the emptying of the Jewish concept of election or the reinterpretation of the *Volksgedanke* into that of the 'ideal human community'.[6] Thus he had nothing but contempt for the liberalism of a Geiger – 'pseudo-historical, pseudo-juristic, pseudo-logical, pseudo-ethical'.[7] It may be conjectured that a certain lack of confidence in the contemporary world would also have deterred Rosenzweig from involving Judaism in the fate of so uncertain an entity and its ideologies of progress. 'Es ist aus mit Europa', he wrote in December, 1919; '. . . European culture is today threatened with collapse' (February 1923).[8] This position would have had some affinity with the cataclysmic consciousness of the *Tannaim*.[9]

As for Hegel and Fichte, already before the First World War Rosenzweig had become disillusioned with their monistic, idealist systems and had replaced their supposed insights by the truths of man's immediate individual experience. He found his spiritual forebears in Schopenhauer, Nietzsche and Kierkegaard.[10] But it is also important to note that in the late philosophy of Schelling lay the onset of the New Thinking, on Rosenzweig's own confession, in so far as Schelling rejected the identity of reason and reality, did not derive the existence of God from ontological proofs but derived being from existence (*Sein von Dasein*).[11] On the publication of Heidegger's *Sein und Zeit* (1927), Rosenzweig hailed in him another bearer of his own 'new thinking', in the line of Hermann Cohen's late work.[12]

Whereas one-dimensional thinking and existence are associated in recent years with the abandonment of Hegelian rationalism (e.g. Marcuse's 'one-dimensional man'), Hegelian rationalism was precisely Rosenzweig's target for its one-dimensional character. Rosenzweig himself espoused and created an open, multi-dimensional world, in contrast to 'the one-dimensionality' of the systems of 1800, at its most clear in the system of Hegelian idealism but also apparent in the work of Fichte and the early Schelling. In such systems, Rosenzweig argued, the individual is not derived from the whole without mediation,

> but is enfolded in his position between the next higher and the next lower, as for example Hegel's 'society' in its position between 'family' and 'state'; the current of the total system flows one and universal through all individual figures. This corresponds exactly to the idealistic world-view; here is the reason for the professional impersonality of the philosophers from Parmenides to Hegel. The concept of the unity of the All leaves open no other possibility of a standpoint than that which is just 'waiting its turn' in the *Problemgeschichte* of philosophy.

Rosenzweig argued that this was why Hegel must make the very history of philosophy the systematic conclusion to philosophy, 'because that final factor that appeared capable of contradicting the unity of the All – the personal standpoint of the individual philosophers – was thereby rendered harmless'.[13]

Hand in hand with the denunciation of systems of philosophical idealism went the denunciation of historical idealism. As a young student at Freiburg, in the autumn of 1908, Rosenzweig already condemned the division between history and life. Meinecke's teaching was 'madly beautiful', he wrote to Hans Ehrenberg, but he also complained that Meinecke 'treats history as though it were a platonic dialogue and not murder and killing, oil-colours, rhyme, dissonance, book prefaces and obeisance'.[14] A few years later Rosenzweig linked Hegel's 'Gang' and Ranke's 'Mär' in a common rejection.[15]

This movement was an integral part of Rosenzweig's 'conversion' to Judaism in 1913 from a position in which he all but succumbed to Christianity.[16] In 1920 when Rosenzweig wrote to Meinecke, to explain his rejection of an academic career, he admitted to a 'collapse' in 1913. 'I realized that the road I was then pursuing was flanked by unrealities.' He declared that the study of history would only feed his 'insatiable hunger for *Gestalten* – a hunger without goal or meaning, driven on solely by its own momentum . . . history to me was a purveyor of *Gestalten*, no more . . .' In this extremity Rosenzweig discovered himself : '. . . my life has fallen under the rule of a "dark drive" ', he wrote, 'which I'm aware that I merely *name* by calling it "my Judaism". The scholarly aspect of this whole process – the conversion of the historian into a philosopher – is only a corollary . . .'[17]

His existentialist affiliations by no means led Rosenzweig to a position of absolute historicity à la Heidegger, for example; Löwith, in a famous article, contrasted the two thinkers as the respective embodiments of temporality and eternity.[18] But the disillusion with systems of monistic idealism did enable Rosenzweig to reach 'eternity'. What applied to philosophy applied equally to the philosophy of history. It was precisely through the evident incapacity of history to serve as an autonomous realm of autonomous facts that Rosenzweig reached a meta-historical position. In so doing, he formulated afresh the eternity of Israel, and, through his challenge to those historians who sought to grasp the eternal in the framework and perspective of change, sought not only to put paid to the category of history altogether as a means to the understanding of Israel, but also to rejoin the traditional world of those to whom Israel's possession of the Law and Israel's unmediated relationship to God made of Israel a people apart. Rosenzweig's rejection of history paralleled the rejection of any integration or even contact between Jewish and non-Jewish existence.[19]

Rosenzweig's *magnum opus, Der Stern der Erlösung* (1921), is on the author's own confession not 'a Jewish book'. It deals with Judaism to no greater extent than with Christianity and hardly more so than with Islam – 'it is merely a system of philosophy'.[20] The presentation of Judaism in terms of this system was deeply influenced by the theory of mythology propounded in the romantic irrationalist philosophy of Schelling in the early part of the nineteenth century. It might be most appropriate to claim that the *Stern* presents Judaism in terms of myth, understood as adogmatic, ahistorical and natural–organic.[21] 'There is no essence of Judaism', Rosenzweig declared, 'that would be a concept. There is only a "Hear, O Israel" '.[22] Judaism is its own definition.

The conquest of history was primarily accomplished by means of an assault on its customary division of past and present. Here Rosenzweig's starting point was Faust's dismissive reply to his famulus : 'Was ihr den Geist der Zeiten heisst, das ist im Grund der Herren eigener Geist, in dem die Zieten sich bespiegeln' – that which you call the spirit of the times is in truth the gentlemen's own spirit in which the times are reflected.[23] In other words the spirit of today had an indispensable part in elucidating the past – 'for nothing in the past stands firm in the way one would willingly believe'. The facts themselves 'are now borne high on the wave of the reflective spirit and now swallowed up. Darkness envelopes whole stretches of history if they cease to excite the interest of the present.' Rosenzweig referred to the facts revealed by Guglielmo Ferrero in the history of ancient Rome, 'which clearly only an eye opened to the class-struggle of our own century could see at all.' Burckhardt likewise, in response to the *Persönlichkeitsglaube* of his own time, uncovered in the Italian Renaissance the classical era of the personality cult.

The spirit of the present, Rosenzweig warned, was not therefore a free agent, arbitrarily choosing from the past what it pleased. It was itself a product of the past, could not escape from its own skin, which it had 'inherited from the same periods of the past whose spirit it sought to cognise', and it could make its selection from the past in no other way 'than by inserting itself into this past' (als indem er sich in diese Vergangenheit einfügt). The spirit must make itself into history in order to be able to reflect on the past from the present, and must see the present itself as an historical epoch. 'But this means that an articulation of epochs enters into history in general, for the simple antithesis – past and present – cannot be final but the past must be articulated in itself into many past presents; only in this way does the present present, in which the gentlemen's own spirit lives, finds its counterpart in the past.'

The articulation of epochs was the means to characterise the spirit of history. Rosenzweig referred to the different way in which German history would appear 'should Potsdam really have been only an episode; differently, for example, than it was seen by Treitschke, to whom it was the peak where all the paths from all the valleys of the past came together.' Similarly, the concept of a Middle Ages could not be grasped until 'a new period thought itself able to extend a fraternal hand to a classical antiquity over a whole "dark" millenium.' To articulate history into epochs was the manner in which the evanescent, intangible essence of spirit made itself a 'body'.

But what applied to the history of the peoples did not apply to the history of the Jews. *Their* history lacked 'epochs', *tout court*. When Rosenzweig turned to Jewish history and discussed the traditional division into an epoch before and after the year 70, the importance of which both Zionists and assimilationists emphasised (though for opposing reasons, each in their own light), he denied the very existence of the division. In the dictum that God had gone into exile with His people he saw an indication, 'under a higher viewpoint', of the unity of the two epochs. For a clearer demonstration he referred to the 'great work' of Graetz. Why, Rosenzweig asked, did Graetz take the unprecedented step of beginning the publication of his History *punkt* with Volume iv, that dealing with the period of the Talmud? Because the 'history-dominating' Talmud overcame the great divide that the year 70 would otherwise have brought about and became 'a bridge on which it was possible to move to and fro'. It became a 'climax' in the sense that it made visible the whole span of Jewish history, past and future. Graetz's choice served Rosenzweig not only as a means to nullify any attempt whatever to divide Jewish history into periods but also to proclaim the indivisibility of Jewish history altogether. We may go further, Rosenzweig proclaims, and through the achievement of the Talmud expound the inefficacy of history as a category through which Jewish existence can be grasped, which is thus set apart from all other existences :

This power of history over national life, that itself is what is here denied; when the articulation into epochs is rendered impotent, so is history; the power of history is broken when the means to its exercise of power, i.e. the epochs, are wrested from its hands; and this is precisely what the Talmud does, putting itself in the place which the year 70 would otherwise have taken in the history of the people. One people – but it is free from the power to which all other people are subject, the power of time; a unique people amongst the peoples, amongst the peoples an eternal people.'

Of the three epochs of exile – the Egyptian, the Babylonian and the present – Rosenzweig saw the Babylonian as the truly formative, fitting the Jewish people for an eternal existence apart, for it saw monotheism become a people's religion (and not that of a mere minority), the prophetic renunciation of political activity in favour of the protection of a great power, the emergence of an unchanging language, law and custom, 'withdrawn from the flux of time', so that any innovation could only acquire validity 'if it can be shown that and how it had already been co-revealed at Sinai, i.e. is no innovation'. Fortified in this way, even the third exile had not brought the end of the Jewish people, 'because Jewish history from its beginning moves from exile to exile and because therefore the spirit of the exile, the alienation from land [*Erdefremdheit*], the struggle of the higher life against decline into the limitations of soil and time, is implanted in this history from its beginning.'

So convinced was Rosenzweig of this argument that even the twin, antithetical phenomena of the third exile – Zionism and assimilationism – each of which mistakenly sought in its own specific way to turn the Jews into a normal people, yet bore the traces of an 'eternal' Judaism. First, Herzl's *Der Judenstaat*, despite its political emphasis and normalising endeavour, had overtones of the ideal state; second, although the assimilationists overwhelmingly sought to eradicate Jewish 'peculiarities', they also, perhaps unwittingly, aspired to bring forth the ideal man.[24]

But why attach this importance to the Talmud? What did the Talmud mean to Rosenzweig? By way of explanation note his regret (in 1921) at not having read Weber's *Das antike Judentum* during the war, for he 'would well have been able to work it into the *Stern* : it is historically the same as what I expressed philosophically'.[25] Weber's work denoted to Rosenzweig the notion of a Jewish existence led within the unchanging framework of rabbinic law, remote from the mainstream of the world's happenings, in the patient expectation of the Messiah.[26]

But what to Weber had a praiseworthy though negative colour was made by Rosenzweig into a positive achievement that encompassed not only a life apart but also an eternal life. If Israel had no history, as Rosenzweig accepted, was this not because Israel lived within the confines of a timeless law?

'Everything of the world has at all times its history; justice and state, art and science, everything that is visible.' But only in that moment when 'the echo of the summons to God's revelation reverberates to man, does a part of temporality die the death-in-resurrection of eternity.'[27] It is revelation alone that creates the possibility of what Rosenzweig called 'the union of our consciousness with the configuration of the world and the heavens stretching beyond the earth'.[28] What Rosenzweig meant by this was the notion that history had, through revelation, acquired a distinct articulation dividing paganism from redemption.[29] Within this schema Judaism enjoyed a unique existence that was both part of the world and separate from it.

What characterised the Jew was his meta-historical stance. Since at least the year 70 he had had no part in the life of the time, of the world, of history. He had stood beyond that life which 'is in time, allows itself to be carried away by the past and calls the future forward'. That is how the nations live but from *that* life of flux – and it is here that the Talmud asserts its supremacy – God withdrew the Jews, 'by spanning above the stream of time the heaven-high bridge of His Law beneath whose vault time now flows powerlessly away to all eternity.'[30] The *Torah* (the teaching and the Law) 'takes the people from out of all the temporality and historicity of life'.[31] To the Law Rosenzweig attributed the power to create for the Jew an unchanging existence, so that 'our eternity makes all the moments of our history simultaneous'.[32] A kiss from Helen made Faustus immortal; the Law, the Jew. Rosenzweig echoed the Mosaic declaration: 'Neither with you only do I make this covenant and this oath; but with him that standeth here with us this day before the Lord our God, and also with him that is not here with us this day' (Deuteronomy XXIX, 14–15).[33]

The effect, if not power, of the Law was accompanied and reinforced in Rosenzweig's view by that of blood, what he termed
'the eternal self-maintenance of reproductive blood'.[34] It was
characteristic of Rosenzweig's method to make motifs and themes
from the Christian opponents of Judaism and turn them to positive
ends.[35] Here he seems to be responding to Hegel's early essay *Der
Geist des Judentums und sein Schicksal* (*c.* 1799) which argued
that when Abraham heeded the divine command to 'Get thee
out of thy country' (Genesis xii, 1ff.) he became, in Hegel's words,
'a stranger on earth, a stranger to soil and men alike'.[36] Indeed
so, Rosenzweig echoed, but this *Erdefremdheit* he saw as the very
condition of eternity. The commandment to Abraham, and the
subsequent periods of exile to Egypt and Babylon, prefigured the
fate of a people that did not base its trust in survival on mere
autochtonous factors, the mere occupation of a certain area, but,
so to speak, bore its eternity with it, in 'the community of blood'.[37]
'We alone trusted to blood and forsook the land.'[38] Rosenzweig
understood this in a very material and physical sense – 'only blood
gives to the hope in the future a guarantee in the present . . . in
the natural propagation of the body does it have the guarantee
of its eternity.'[39] So much emphasis is given by Rosenzweig to the
idea of biological continuity that it is to be regarded as the saving
counterpart to the degeneration that attachment to the land
would otherwise entail. The one preserves, the other destroys.

The biological argument – indeed, reality – also reinforced, the
idea of eternity. It made all the time-separated generations into
one. It brought about an 'alliance' between ancestor and descend-
ant who saw 'in each other in the same moment the latest grandson and the first ancestor. Thus the grandson and the ancestor,
both in each other, and both together for him who stands between
them, are the true embodiment of the eternal people.'[40]

Rosenzweig developed his reading of the eternality of Jewish
life so that it came to constitute a closed circle, immune and im-
previous to ordinary time. The weekly celebration of the Sabbath,
for example, already heralds redemption. It is the festival of a
creation that took place for the very sake of redemption, 'the
meaning and goal of creation'. During the ten days of penitence
between the New Year and the Day of Atonement, 'the year
wholly becomes the fully-valid representative of eternity', in whose
yearly recurrence eternity is freed from all 'the remoteness of the

beyond' (jenseitige Ferne) and becomes 'real and manifest'. Similarly, the Jewish calendar is itself coeval with the very creation of the world and does not reckon from any merely historical event. As for the pilgrim festival of the Passover, Rosenzweig echoes the Talmudic dictum (Mishnah Pesahim, x, 5) that each and every celebrant must feel as though he himself had taken part in the Exodus from Egypt. Likewise, only to outward appearance are the Feast of Weeks and the Feast of Tabernacles 'festivals of remembrance' – 'in truth the historical in them is a quite dense present'. Here again each celebrant must feel that he was *himself* present at the events they commemorate. Even those ceremonies and occasions that do explicitly and expressly commemorate *historical* events – the destruction of the Temple, the rededication of the Temple, and the deliverance celebrated in the Book of Esther – the events that they each year recall have become 'rigid – like the history of the people'.[41]

Thus the Jew lived spiritually, and even physically, within a past that was eternally recalled and renewed in the present. For Rosenzweig, to be a Jew was to live within the framework of an existence bounded by what had been revealed at Sinai and a relative time scale of later events. The biological continuity, the dominion of the Law, the jump across the irrelevant and meaningless centuries – all this connoted a phenomenon that had renounced any active historical participatory role for the sake of its commitment to an eternal life within the world of temporality. This renunciation is the price that Judaism has paid and must continue to pay for its meta-historical existence.

The Jewish world is alive with paradoxes, polarities and contradictions. God is both the God of retribution and the God of love. Israel knows that it is the elect of God but that also to Egypt and Assyria God says: 'my people'. The man of the beginning – Adam – confronts the man of the end – the Messiah; the first miracles stand against the last, which, it is said, will be greater than the first.

The workaday Jewish world is itself built up of the same contradiction or coexistence of present and future, in that it belongs to both. It suffers from a fundamental ambivalence, e.g. an object can be 'ensouled' through the utterance of a benediction which has a twofold purpose: in 'this' world the object serves an everyday use, hardly otherwise than if no benediction had been pronounced, but it is now at the same time one of the stones from which the 'coming' world will be constructed. 'Blessing splits the world, in order to make it whole again in the future, but for the present only the split is visible.' The split penetrates the whole of life, embodying the contrast between holy and profane, Sabbath and work-day, '*Torah* and the way of the world', spiritual life and livelihood.[42]

But the world of the Jew does not remain in the divided state. The polarity or contradiction is only evident if that world is viewed through a quest for essence – 'but living life does not ask for essence'. It lives, and in so doing answers all questions before they can even be posed.[43]

The dimension of time remains, though not in the guise of *historical* time as commonly understood. It coexists with eternity, so far as the Jew is concerned. What takes place is not a transposition but a trans-valuation of the beginning and the end – the beginning has not yet taken place whereas the end has already happened. 'That is Judaism : the beginning of the *Zwischenreich*, the coming of the Messiah, has not yet been; the end, the Kingdom of God, has already begun, is already there, exists today already for each Jew in the direct conclusive relationship to God himself, in the daily "taking on to oneself" of the yoke of the Kingdom of Heaven through the fulfilment of the Law.' This is a reference to R. Nehunya ben Hakanah's dictum : 'whosoever assumes the yoke of the *Torah*, they remove from him the yoke of government and the yoke of worldly affairs' (*Pirkei Avoth*, III, 5).[44] In other words, the two basic constituents dominating the Jew's awareness of time are : (*a*) the messiah has not yet come, *but* (*b*) the kingdom of God is already real.[45]

The matter does not end there. The world of the Jew does not remain in its divided state. The paradox – if paradox it be – of the coexistence of history and eternity – is resolved through the practice of the Law and the world is made whole again. The Law appeases and overcomes the unease born of the thought that the world is both created and yet in need of future redemption. In its manysidedness and power the Law has an ordering capacity that comprehends all 'external' life, i.e. the life of this world, everything that a secular justice can grasp, and thereby 'makes this world and the next indistinguishable'. All created existence is given life and soul in the Law as the direct content of the future world. Furthermore, and by way of completion and climax, the bond between human action and fulfilment is mediated through the Law, the performance by the Jew of the 'endless customs and precepts for the sake of "uniting the holy God and His Shekhinah".' The glory of God, dispersed in countless sparks throughout the world, will be reunited. 'Each of his [the Jew's] acts, each fulfilment of the Law completes a part of this union . . . for this unity, it is while it becomes, it is becoming into unity.'[46]

In this way Rosenzweig transforms the category of history and of the present into a phenomenon the meaning of which is not immanent but derived from a point beyond history – that of revelation. But it is not a point beyond the reach of the Jew. The Jew, through the fulfilment of the Law, is the instrument for the redemption of the historical world into the kingdom of heaven. Through him, the present and the future become one.

Rosenzweig's presentation of Judaism is illuminated through the confrontation with Christianity, 'on a sociological basis', in the *Stern der Erlösung*.[47] As elsewhere, he takes a negative Christian symbol of Judaism and turns it round to yield a positive content. He takes the medieval juxtaposition of the blindfold synagogue and its broken staff, with its counterpart, the church militant, 'eyes open to the world, sure of victory'.[48] To Rosenzweig this signified the withdrawal of the synagogue from time, the world and history, its glance fixed on eternity – as against the church, 'in the midst of the event'.[49] Whilst declaring that the tension in the synthesis between the church and the world was 'fruitful', a synthesis to which Christian Europe owed 'its spiritual predominance in the world', he also pointed out that Christianity had found this tension 'tormenting', as something to be avoided.[50] By virtue of the Christian's involvement in the world he must experience the discord between Christ and 'Siegfried', between priest and saint, between church and state. His law is forever changing as a result of revolutions whereas that of the Jew is impervious to time – 'he may well escape it but not change it'. In the last resort, whereas the Jew enjoys 'the inner harmony of belief and life', there is, in the life of the peoples, a contradiction (though it is a 'motive power' in their life) 'between uniqueness and world history, homeland and belief, earth and heaven'.[51] The Jew knows that 'inner harmony of faith and life' which St Augustine, in 'the harmony of *fides* and *salus* may well ascribe to the church, but which remains to the peoples in the church a mere dream'.[52]

In personal terms Rosenzweig juxtaposed Christian faith with the Jew *as* faith. The Jew by birth confronts the Christian, to whom faith must be brought from outside. The Christian's faith in something is precisely the contrary of the Jew's faith which Rosenzweig punningly calls 'not the content of a testimony [Zeugnis] but the product of a reproduction' [Erzeugnis einer Zeugung].[53] A Jew is born, a Christian made. Christianus fit, non nascitur.[54] The man who must be baptised before he becomes a Christian confronts the man who is a Jew before he is even born.

This introduced Rosenzweig's analysis of anti-semitism and the Christian's hostility to the Jew, to both of which he ascribed a 'meta-physical basis'.[55] Not only must his faith be brought to the Christian from outside; not only does the Christian suffer from the divergence between his faith and his life; yet more galling, as Rosenzweig saw it, was the Christian's awareness of his position in time as against the position of the Jew beyond time – 'his world has reached its target' – a target to which the peoples of the world 'are striving'.[56]

If the Jew belongs to eternity, then the Christian belongs to time; if the Jew is at the end of history and thereby beyond history, then the Christian is forever on the way. He is forever moving towards a position that the Jew forever occupies. To the Christian 'every event stands midway between the beginning and end of the eternal path and is by virtue of this middle position itself eternal in the temporal *Zwischenreich* of eternity'.[57]

This antithesis makes the Jew 'the eternal *enfant terrible*', 'the obstinate mute admonisher'. His mere presence at all times serves to recall to the Christian that he has not and will not reach his goal of truth, but is forever on the way. The rejection of the Jew by Christianity is therefore, in the final, metaphysical analysis, 'only self-hatred, hatred of its own imperfection, of its own not-yet'.[58]

The Jew, says Rosenzweig, is 'at one with himself' (ganz bei sich).[59] He achieves this self-identity through his withdrawal from the world of change, history and so forth, and through his individual cleaving to the timeless, eternal world of the *Torah*.

The idea of the Jews as an eternal people is sanctified by tradition; likewise, the idea that the revelation at Sinai was an event central to the history of the world. Rosenzweig of course accepted these propositions. But whereas they had previously been invested with the notion of the conquest of time and the world, Rosenzweig altogether devalued the notion of time and the world. This was only attained at the cost of the emasculation of the Law. The Law, in the classic formulation of Maimonides, 'aims at two things : the welfare of the soul and the welfare of the body'. These ends, Maimonides further emphasises, are inseparable from 'a political association . . . The true Law . . . has come to bring us both perfections, I mean the welfare of the states of people in their relation with one another through the abolition of reciprocal wrongdoing and through the acquisition of a noble and excellent character.'[60] But if the Jew is, as Rosenzweig postulated, removed from the world of history, politics, etc. then the Law as a whole is nullified, abandoned to a vacuum where it can only expire. It can take no grip of reality. Rosenzweig here approached the liberal Judaism which was otherwise anathema to him.[61] He introduced thereby a bifurcation between physical and spiritual life as great, perhaps, as any in the Christian world. He himself wrote, for example, of the Jewish people, 'its soul, which is satiated in the contemplation of hope, is dead to labour, action, the struggle for the world. The consecration, with which it is anointed as a kingdom of priests, makes its life unfruitful; its holiness prevents it from giving up its soul to the yet unhallowed world of the peoples, however much it may be attached to this world with its body.'[62] Thus, although Rosenzweig does indeed emphasise the phsysical world of the Jew in terms of biological continuity, he places large areas of that physical world beyond the dominion of the Law, and thereby deprives the Law of its *raison d'être*. It is necessary to challenge Rosenzweig's presentation of an Abraham summoned to leave his land in order that he should, in spirit alone, enter the kingdom of heaven but leave his politics behind. How, then, can a Jew be 'at one with himself?' When R. Nehunyah b. Hakanah said, 'whoever assumes the yoke of the Law, they remove from him the yoke of government and the yoke of worldly affairs'[63] did he intend to abandon 'government' and 'worldly affairs' to some uncertain realm without the Law? Assuredly not, for precisely these areas are a principal concern of the Law.

Rosenzweig argued that, as an essential part of its freedom from history, what distinguished Israel – constituted indeed its great title to distinction – was its separation from the land : 'we preserved the precious sap of life, which offered us a guarantee of our own eternity and, alone amongst all the peoples of the world, freed our vitality from that communion with the dead. For the soil nourishes, but it also binds . . .'[64] If Rosenzweig did indeed cite the prophets to support his contention that Israel must refuse to descend to the level of the other peoples and seek 'participation in the political dealings of the world', he also forbore to take account of the prophetic lament at Israel's loss of sovereignty : 'for a voice of wailing is heard out of Zion – "How are we undone! We are greatly confounded, because we have forsaken the land, Because our dwellings have cast us out".' (Jeremiah ix, 18). By the waters of Babylon the psalmist may have sat down and wept, but not Rosenzweig. On the contrary, the Babylonian exile, coming between the Egyptian and the present, was picked out by Rosenzweig as that period of special value which became 'the true training ground of Judaism' – when pure monotheism became a religion of the majority and 'the dream of a political independence' was finally dispersed. From now on it was Israel's destiny to live under the protection of a great power – Persia, in actual fact, following the return from Babylon. Admittedly, Rosenzweig continued, a kingdom was renewed under the rule of the Maccabees, 'but it remained a mere name, with independence a highly precarious affair, a gift of the Roman overlords.'[65] Israel was 'a more faithful servant to its land' when it tarried beyond its borders, 'and yearns for the lost homeland . . . In the deepest sense the land is precisely its own as the land of its yearnings, as – a holy land.'[66] Rosenzweig was no Zionist[67] and it seems that he was able to visualise political independence, and thereby participation in historical life, purely in terms of the, to him, unwelcome realisation of Zionism. Be that as it may, what Rosenzweig took from the prophets and the Biblical teachings generally was only the injunction not to go 'whoring after false gods' and not the complementary obligation and injunction to construct the ideal society.

In his essay *Die Bauleute* (1923), directed against Buber's *Reden über das Judentum*, Rosenzweig did indeed subject 'our whole being' to the commitment to the Law, quoting the Midrashic image of the compulsion exercised by God at Sinai.[68] But this strengthened concept remained undefined.

A more serious objection must arise from the very notion of an unchanging Law. It can, for example, hardly have escaped Rosenzweig's attention that the Law was very differently understood and expounded in the Talmud, than, say, in the philosophies of Philo, Maimonides and Hermann Cohen. It could not therefore serve as that 'heaven-high bridge . . . beneath whose vault time now flows powerlessly away to all eternity'. On the contrary, what distinguished the Law was precisely its involvement in the life of time and history : its flexibility and capacity to bring an infinity of changing circumstances within its grasp. Rosenzweig was himself not consistent in respect of the 'unchanging' Law. At a time when 'European culture threatened to collapse', and required, he once declared, help from 'supra-European and supra-human powers', of which Judaism was one, 'the eternity of these powers is preserved in their ability to secularize themselves again and again'.[69] He further admitted that only by a sort of fiction can it be shown that 'there are no legislators who renewed the Law in the living course of time . . . even what is perhaps innovation in substance must yet always present itself as though it already stood in the eternal Law and was co-revealed in its revelation.'[70] It may well be possible to argue that some substance or essence or kernel of the law lives unchanged amidst change in form or accident. But nothing of this is evident in Rosenzweig.

Rosenzweig presented a paradoxical picture of the Jew who lives, strictly speaking, at a point in time that he has not reached, who, by virtue of the fact that he is on way, has also reached his destination. This privileged position gave to the Jew his status as the *enfant terrible* of the world in general and the Christian world in particular. From his position at the end of time he served as a perpetual reminder and goad to the world that what it was forever striving to achieve he had himself already attained. But this attempt to make of Judaism a supra-temporal phenomenon with a corresponding detachment from land and history must be accounted a failure. Not only does it discard the traditional notion of a historical God but it also fails to take account of that perpetual striving that involved Judaism in the historical world with a view to its actual transformation.

9 Conclusion

If the *idée-maîtresse* of Jewish historical thinking is concern not with the past but with the future; if it values the past merely for what it can convey of the future – then such thinking must be essentially an ambiguous undertaking. If, as Graetz argued, Judaism, on the model of the prophets, 'struggles for a present that it lacks',[1] then it cannot interest itself in the world of history for that would be to deify the transient; yet it must, on the other hand, acknowledge that it is precisely in that transient historical world that God has made known His revelation, and from that world the messianic future is to be constructed or, at least, to emerge.

The use of history to divine the future was the occasion for multiple rabbinical reprobation. At its most extreme, those who sought to calculate the date of the coming of the messiah were the object of Talmudic imprecation, as much for sociological reasons as for the impiety involved in the attempt to discern the intention of God : 'people would say, since the predetermined time has come, but he has not, he will never come'.[2] In more recent times, the messianic idea has been seen, not as the completion of history, but, almost, as its negation. Scholem for example, has written of the 'price', in terms of historical life, that the messianic idea has exacted from Judaism. He continues :

the greatness of the messianic idea corresponds to the infinite weakness of Jewish history which in exile was not ready to engage itself at the historical level. It has the weakness of the temporary, or the provisional that does not spend its strength. For the messianic idea is not only solace and hope. In every attempt at its realization the abysses break open which lead each of its figures *ad absurdum*. To live in hope is something great but it is also something deeply unreal. It devalues the weight of the person who can never fulfil himself . . . Thus the messianic idea in Judaism has forced *life into suspense* in which nothing can be done or achieved in a final way . . . The messianic idea, it may be said, is the genuinely anti-existentialist idea.[3]

None the less, in a desultory, inconclusive way, the Talmud does itself present a number of dynamic models, aprioristically conceived, that embody the messianic process.[4] There is the 'catastrophe' view which speaks of the 'birth pangs' of the messiah and identifies the onset of the messianic age with lack of charity, poverty, dissolution of family ties, disrespect for the law, etc.[5] This, in modern times, has its obvious counterpart in the thinking of Abrabanel, say, whom the very expulsion from Spain and Portugal inspired with the vision of a redeemed Israel, raised from the dust amidst a mighty conflict between Christendom and Islam in the sixteenth century. Not essentially different was the picture of Hermann Cohen. *His* cataclysmic conflict was the First World War. 'From distress' he saw 'a new virtue' growing, in which the idea of the state 'ripens into the League of Nations. Messianism is becoming a factor in world history.'[6]

A second Talmudic model of the end of days speaks of the six thousand years that the world will endure – two thousand years of desolation, two thousand when the *Torah* flourishes and two thousand during which the messiah will come.[7] This schema may in its turn be likened, *toutes proportions gardées*, to that of those historians (e.g. Graetz and Krochmal) who seem to have identified Judaism's enhanced self-consciousness as a condition of the advent of the messianic era. A third model, in the name of R. Johanan, encompasses all positions : 'the son of David will come only in a generation that is either altogether righteous or altogether wicked'.[8]

That the Talmud should refrain from enunciating a firm conclusion need occasion no surprise. It is at least wiser in that respect than those historians who invested a passing historical conjunction with eschatological significance or sought to divine the future from the past. The superior wisdom showed itself even more dramatically not only in the quasi-refusal to entertain visions of the future except in fanciful terms, but also in the determination to subject history to its own standard procedure, i.e. distrusting the unique and emphasising the general, and thus transmuting history into prescription.

The concentration on elaborating the means as opposed to luxuriating in the ends is the precise reversal of the utopian thinking common to the Gentile world. Where is that rabbinic Republic, that rabbinic City of the Sun, Phalanstery, New Atlantis, Oceana, etc.? They barely exist because their place is taken by the reality that characterises the existence and activity of the Jewish community. As against this, it has been truly said of More's Utopia (and might be said of most, if not all) that 'it is nowhere, not only geographically, but historically as well. It exists neither in the past nor in the future' – indeed, News from Nowhere. Where the attempt has been made to realise a utopia in a particular historical setting – e.g. those Brook Farms, Icarias, Oneidas – their very fragility only emphasises the contrast with the sustained, though often erroneous, Jewish endeavour.

It has also truly been said of Utopia that the 'realization [of its institutions] is scarcely mentioned'.[9] Such constructions can therefore be nothing more than instruments for the critique of the existing. The strength of the Talmud's use of history lies precisely in the fact that it makes possible the advance from critique to *praxis*.[10] It thus averts the degeneration of historiography into what Nietzsche called 'a picture gallery'.

As against this contribution of the Talmud, what can history offer, especially the messianological history of the mode practised by the historians discussed earlier? Only fantasy. It is true of course that none of the historians here discussed (apart from Dubnow) separated the messianic idea from its halakhic instrumentalism and ground. Yet all that they too could offer was fantasy. This faculty, it is true, does preserve an objective from oblivion and facilitate the perception of something that is not yet present.[11] But it cannot go beyond the mere perception. If history, with its inseparable element of fantasy, is not to be dismissed altogether, it is again necessary to have recourse to the Talmud for that missing practical factor. Here that model proclaimed by R. Judah is relevant: 'if Israel were to keep two Sabbaths according to the laws thereof, they would be redeemed immediately . . .'[12] If, therefore, as S. R. Hirsch argued, the purpose of its history is to refine and prepare Israel for the fulfilment of the *Torah*,[13] then the notion of *praxis* can serve to bring what might otherwise degenerate into a museum exhibit or a fantasy beneath 'the yoke of the *Torah*'. Here is the inspiration of an historical understanding that will look on the history of the Jews in the light of their relationship to the fulfilment of the messianic task. If, as the rabbis argued, the world only exists by virtue of the *Torah*, then the historian will require to know how successfully that incommensurable burden is being borne by those to whom it has been entrusted.

Notes

Preface

1 Y. Wolfsberg, *Mkoma shel ha'Historiya ba'filosofiya ha'datit*, I, pt 4 (Sinai, 1938) pp. 440–1.

2 Werblowsky has written, for example:

> In general it can be said that the historical, national reference of the Messianic faith has been preserved in most theological writings. Redemption, whatever else it may mean, always also means the actual physical liberation of Israel from persecution and humiliation, its return to its ancient homeland, the restoration of the Davidic dynasty, the rebuilding of the Temple in Jerusalem and the recognition by all nations of Israel's election and calling. Whatever the spiritual significances attached to these hopes, they were never allowed to dissolve the concrete historical core into pure spirituality. The reality of Israel's historic consciousness and, we may add, the reality of anti-semitism, saw to it that the spiritual or mystical 'interiorizations' of Judaism never lost their touch with reality; redemption from evil and sin was always regarded as connected with the conquest of evil in the historical, that is, the political and social spheres.

'Judaism, or the Religion of Israel', in R. C. Zaehner (ed.), *The Concise Encyclopaedia of Living Faiths* (London, 1959) pp. 47–8; see also Erwin I. J. Rosenthal, 'Vom Geschichtlichen Fortleben des Judentums', in W. Strolz (ed.), *Jüdische Hoffnungskraft, Geschichtsbewusstsein und Christlicher Glaube* (Freiburg, 1971) p. 28.

3 S. W. Baron, *A Social and Religious History of the Jews*, 2nd ed. (New York, 1952) I, p. 7.

4 A. Altmann, 'Gishot Shonot la'historiya ha'Yisraelit', *Yad Sha'ul*, ed. Weinberg and Biberfeld (Tel Aviv, 1953) p. 134.

E

Chapter 1

1 *Shevet Yehudah, Ha'Shmad Ha'Shlishi*, ed. A. Shohat (repr. Jerusalem, 1947); see also pp. 37ff below. With a sure instinct did Marc Bloch pointedly not include the Jews amongst 'the history-writing peoples' (*Apologie pour l'histoire*, Paris, 1949, p. ix).

2 I. M. Jost, *Geschichte des Judentums und Seiner Secten* (Leipzig, 1859) iii, p. 279. (For Gans' work see below, pp. 44ff.)

3 *Bikkurei Ha'Ittim*, x (1829) p. iv.

4 *Kitve*, ed. S. Rawidowicz (London, 1961) p. 202.

5 Ibid., pp. 7–9.

6 Ibid., pp. 143–4.

7 From Krochmal's introduction to the 'Guide', ibid., p. 5.

8 Ibid., p. 149.

9 Ibid., p. 209.

10 Rawidowicz, Introduction (*Mevo*) to the *Kitve*, p. 158.

11 S. Maimon, *Autobiography*, Eng. trans. (London, 1957) p. 135.

12 L. Zunz, *Literaturgeschichte der synagogalen Poesie* (Berlin, 1865) p. 1; note also Zunz's pungent comment: 'lacking a state, therefore an historical unit' (*Gesammelte Schriften*, ed. M. Brann, Vol. i, Frankfurt a.M., 1908, p. 136); cf. David Kaufman: 'With the collapse of an independent history, historical writing had also come to an end amongst the Jews' (*Gesammelte Schriften*, p. 274); Simon Bernfeld: 'After the destruction of the Second Temple, historical consciousness utterly ceased in Israel' ('Dorshei Reshumot', Ha'Shiloah, ii, Apr–Sept 1899, 193); A. A. Neuman: 'The art of historic writing among the Jews came to a sudden and abrupt end with the destruction of the Jewish state in Palestine . . . all interest in history was abandoned. In the national shipwreck, every secular literary interest was submerged' (*The Shebet Yehudah and Sixteenth-Century Historiography*, Louis Ginzberg Jubilee Volume, English Section, New York, 1945, p. 255); see also J. Meisl, *Graetz, eine Würdigung* (Berlin, 1917) p. 27; A. I. Agus, *Al Historiografiya shel Yisrael ba'golah*, S. K. Mirsky Jubilee Volume, ed. Bernstein and Churgin (Hebrew Section) (New York, 1958) p. 441; and B. D. Weinryb, *Reappraisals in Jewish History*, S. W. Baron Jubilee Volume, ii (Jerusalem, 1974) pp. 943–4. Baron attributes historical apathy to Israel's lack of 'political' history, in the ordinary sense, to the supreme power of the Law, 'which suffered no rivals', and to the continuous migrations which interrupted continuity

and increasingly obstructed the preservation of historical records (*Social and Religious History of the Jews*, I, p. 26); cf. also Morris Cohen, 'Philosophies of Jewish History', *Jewish Social Studies*, I, no. 1 (Jan 1939) 40. E. Bickermann writes: 'un oubli général couvrit les siècles qui s'étaient écoulés entre Alexandre et Auguste, parce que personne n'avait plus intérêt à s'en souvenir . . . Après Hérode et surtout sur les ruines du Temple, qui pouvait avoir de l'intérêt pour un Judas Maccabée?' ('La Chaîne de la tradition pharisienne', *Revue Biblique*, LIX, 1952, 45–7).

13 M. Hess, *Die Europäische Triarchie* (Leipzig, 1841) p. 112.

14 *Rom und Jerusalem*, Vorwort: for the negative (although ambivalent) attitude of Zionist thinking to the Jewish past see also E. Schweid's remarks in the symposium reported in *Hakarat He'Avar* (Jerusalem, 1969) pp. 146–7.

15 S. Holdheim, *Das Ceremonialgesetz im Messiasreich* (Schwerin, 1845) pp. 125ff.

16 See below, pp. 93ff.

17 Gavin Langmuir, 'Majority History and Post-Biblical Jews', *Journal of the History of Ideas*, 27 (1966) 343. See also G. F. Moore, 'Christian Writers on Judaism', *Harvard Theological Review*, XIV (1921) 197–254, and the very important work of Rosemary Ruether, *Faith and Fratricide* (London, 1975) *passim*.

18 M. Weber, *Gesammelte Aufsätze zur Religionssoziologie*, III (Tübingen, 1923) p. 442; see also J. Guttmann, 'Max Webers Soziologie des antiken Judentums', *Monatsschrift für die Geschichte und Wissenschaft des Judentums*, 69, NF 33 (1925); Freddy Raphael, 'Weber and Judaism', *Leo Baeck Year Book*, XVIII (1973) esp. pp. 59–60; for other evaluations of the general theme see H. Liebeschütz, 'Max Weber's Historical Interpretation of Judaism', ibid., IX (1964) 41–68; and the contributions by Taubes and Maier to *Max Weber and Sociology Today*, ed. Otto Stammer (Oxford, 1971) pp. 187–96.

19 *Gesammelte Aufsätze zur Wissenschaftslehre* (Tübingen, 1951) p. 597.

20 *A Study of History* (Oxford, 1933) I, pp. 35, 51; V, p. 8. On this see N. Rotenstreich, *The Recurring Pattern* (London, 1963) ch. 4; also H. M. Orlinsky, 'On Toynbee's Use of the Term Syriac for One of His Societies', *In the Time of Harvest, Essays in Honour of Abba Hillel Silver* (New York, 1963) pp. 255–69; Peter Kaupp, 'Toynbee and the Jews', *Wiener Library Bulletin*, XXI, no. 1 (winter 1966–7).

Chapter 2

1 See below, p. 106.

2 *Genesis Rabbah*, I, 6; *Leviticus Rabbah*, XXXVI, 4; *Talmud Babli Ta'anith*, 3b (hereafter cited as *T.B.*).

3 *Genesis Rabbah*, IX, 2.

4 *T.B. Shabbath*, 88a; see also *Deuteronomy Rabbah*, VIII, 5; *Ruth Rabbah* (intro), 1; *Avoda Zara*, 5a.

5 See Israel Abrahams, *A Companion to the Authorised Daily Prayer Book* (London, 1922) pp. lix, 159. Wiener writes: 'the Biblical-Jewish God is from the outset experienced as that which rules history. He creates the world only as an arena for the actions of men' ('Aufriss einer jüdischen Theologie', *Hebrew Union College Annual*, XVIII, 1943–4, 376).

6 Altmann, op. cit., p. 133.

7 Acknowledgement for the following analysis is gratefully made to N. Glatzer, *Untersuchungen zur Geschichtslehre der Tannaiten* (Berlin, 1932).

8 *T.B. Berakhoth*, 3a.

9 *Pesikta de Rav Kahana*, ed. S. Buber (Lyck, 1868) p. 151a.

10 Deuteronomy IV, 23, 32; VII, 18; XXXII, 7; Isaiah XLVI, 9–10. See also A. Momigliano, 'Time in Ancient Historiography', *History and Theory*, Beiheft 6 (1966) esp. pp. 19ff. It is highly important to note that the Hebrew term for 'remember' has a power lacking to its English counterpart, i.e. 'memory' not only establishes the continuity between past and present but also enables those who properly remember to participate again in the past, e.g. the Exodus. 'Memory functions as an actualisation (Vergegenwärtigung) of the decisive event' in the tradition of Israel (see B. S. Childs, *Memory and Tradition in Israel*, Studies in Biblical Theology, no. 37 (London, 1962) pp. 50ff).

11 *T.B. Pesahim*, 116b.

12 J. Lestchinsky, 'Do Jews Learn From History?', *Jewish Journal of Sociology*, V, no. 2, p. 245. The *herem* on Spain is considered an exception (ibid., p. 246).

13 *T.B. Berakhoth*, 13a.

14 Glatzer, op. cit., p. 34. For other uses of the past that partially overlap with those described here, see J. H. Plumb, *The Death of the Past* (London, 1969) Parts I and II.

15 The findings of social psychology confirm that frustrated expectations of reality can to a large extent be compensated for by a firm social anchorage (see e.g. Hans Albert, *Plädoyer für kritischen Rationalismus*, Munich, 1971, pp. 30ff).

16 *Exodus Rabbah,* xix, 7; see also Glatzer, op. cit., pp. 37–8.
17 R. R. Geis, 'Das Geschichtsbild des Talmud', *Saeculum,* vi (1955) 121.
18 *Song of Songs Rabbah,* i, 8.
19 *T.B. Pesahim,* 118b.
20 *Ecclesiastes Rabbah,* iii, 16. (Tineius Rufus was the Roman governor of Judea at the time of the martydom of R. Akiba in 135 c.e.)
21 *Lamentations Rabbah,* ii, 2.
22 *Pesikta de Rav Kahana,* p. 120b.
23 *T. B. Makkoth,* pp. 24a–b.
24 *Pesikta,* p. 123b.
25 *Emunoth Ve'Deoth,* ch. vii, 1.
26 *Hegels theologische Jugendschriften,* ed. H. Nohl (Tübingen, 1907) pp. 214ff.
27 In a letter to Jan Ehrenwald in 1937 (see 'The Jews of Czechoslovakia', ii, *JPSA,* 1971, 468).
28 *Religion der Vernunft aus den Quellen des Judentums* (Leipzig, 1919) pp. 308, 293.
29 *Leviticus Rabbah,* xxvii, 4; see also Glatzer, op. cit., pp. 123–5.
30 And not only the historian. Zunz shows that from the tenth century onward there existed a continuing tradition of calculating 'the end of time' (despite all rabbinic disapproval and prohibition) and that barely a decade passed that did not contain a year designated by one calculator or another as that when the redeemer was to appear ('Erlösungsjahre', *Gesammelte Schriften,* iii, Berlin, 1876, pp. 224–31).
31 J. Neusner, 'Religious Uses of History', *History and Theory,* v, no. 2 (1966) 170. Although Glatzer speaks of 'meta-history', 'extra-history', etc. in the Weber–Rosenzweig fashion, it does not seem that he is seriously at variance with Neusner. He writes of a similar displacement of the messianic idea from the active to the peaceful, from the 'urgent expectation of change into distant, quiet hope; from a history-centred doctrine into a meta-historical one'. ('The Attitude towards Rome in Third Century Judaism', *Politische Ordnung und Menschliche Existenz – Festgabe für E. Voegelin,* Munich, 1962, pp. 242–57.) 'Messianic protest against Rome was replaced by a life of concentration on Sinai and its message . . . The same century that witnessed Christianity enter into an alliance with Rome and emerge into the bright light of history saw Israel developing a theory of extra-historical existence' (p. 257).
32 See *T.B. Sotah,* 35a. Somewhat less than a millenium later

Maimonides echoed this critique when he juxtaposed and disparaged those who think they 'understand a book that is the guide of the first and the last men while glancing through it as you would glance through a historical work or a piece of poetry' (*Guide to the Perplexed*, I, 2, trans. Pines). Hermann Cohen writes of the 'one-sidedness' of the interest in the one God : 'not drama, also not lyric poetry in the sense of the erotic, no binding of the intellectual to eros . . . everywhere the repression of poetry by the problems of ethical teaching, everywhere therefore the direction and limitation of the human to the association of men, but a turning away from the egoistic. Thus poetry itself leads towards messianism' (op. cit., p. 301).

33   'Poetry is more philosophical and more weighty than history, for poetry speaks rather of the universal, history of the particular. By the universal I mean that such or such a kind of man will say or do such or such things from probability or necessity; that is the aim of poetry, adding proper names to the characters. By the particular I mean what Alcibiades did, or what he suffered' (*Poetics*, IX); Neusner, op. cit., p. 153 suggests the comparison. It seems that in this respect the Talmud allied itself to that mode of rationalist thought, running from Aristotle to Descartes (*Discours de la Méthode*), Spinoza (*Tractatus*) and Mendelssohn which denies to the raw material of history the status of knowledge; see also L. Lazar, *Die Geschichtsauffassung der Propheten in Verhältnis zur Geschichtsphilosophie des Idealismus der Gegenwart* (Lodz, 1935) p. 7.

34   *T.B. Kiddushin*, 2a–b; *Baba Bathra*, 69a–b.

35   See the references cited in M. Elon, *Ha'Mishpat Ha'Ivri* (Jerusalem, 1973) I, p. 191.

36   Glatzer, op. cit., pp. 44ff.

37   See M. Weber, *Gesammelte Aufsätze zur Religionssoziologie,* III (Tübingen, 1923) p. 6.

38   H. H. Ben-Sasson, 'L'Magamot ha'Kronografiya ha'Yehudit shel ymei ha'beinayim u'Bayoteha', *Historiyonim v'askolot historiyot* (Jerusalem, 1962) pp. 29–49.

39   *Pirkei Avoth*, I. This was the very model of a traditional society that conceived its past 'as an immemorial continuity, its structure as inherited from an infinitely receding chain of transmitters' (J. G. A. Pocock, *Politics, Language and Time*, London, 1972, p. 238).

40   *Ecclesiastes Rabbah*, I, 10; *T.B. Berakhoth*, 5a; cf. also Elon, op. cit., p. 224.

41   *T.B. Sanhedrin*, 38b; *Avoda Zara*, 5a.

42　A. Funkenstein, 'Gesetz und Geschichte : Zur historisierenden Hermeneutik bei Moses Maimonides und Thomas von Aquin', *Viator*, 1 (1970).

43　*T.B. Menahoth*, 29b.

44　Ed. B. Ratner (Vilna, 1897).

45　See M. Grossberg, introduction to *Seder Olam Zuta* (London, 1910) p. 12.

46　*Literaturgeschichte der synagogalen Poesie* (Berlin, 1865) pp. 1–2.

Chapter 3

1　In fact, Elias Tcherikower ('Jewish Martyrology and Jewish Historiography', *Yivo Annual of Jewish Social Science*, i, New York, 1946, 9–23) saw in those very elegies, martyrologies, dirges and polemical writings a worthy substitute for the 'very inconspicuous place' occupied by historical writings proper, in relation to the multitude of legal codes, scriptural and Talmudic commentaries, theological and philosophical works, rabbinical responsa, etc.; see also A. N. Neubauer, *Medieval Jewish Chronicles* (repr. Amsterdam, 1970).

2　Ed. A. M. Habermann (Jerusalem, 1970).

3　R. Chazan, 'R. Ephraim of Bonn's Sefer Zekhira', *Revue des Etudes Juives*, cxxxii (Jan–June 1973) fasc. 1–2. As a boy of thirteen R. Ephraim took refuge in the citadel of Wolkenburg near Cologne during the second crusade.

4　M. A. Shulvass, *'Ha'Yedia b'Historiya ve'ha'Sifrut ha'historit bi'Tkhum ha'Tarbut shel ha'Yahadut ha'Ashkenazit bi'ymei ha'beinayim'*, Sefer Ha'Yovel le'R. H. Albeck (Jerusalem, 1963) p. 465.

5　Ed. M. Grossberg (London, 1910); see also M. Steinschneider, *Die Geschichtsliteratur der Juden* (Frankfurt, 1905) p. 12, para. 11.

6　Chapter iv in the Grossberg edition.

7　There is an extract from these instructions in Baron, op. cit., vi, pp. 30–1. They read in part as follows :

> Wherever the Talmud expressly leaves open the decision between conflicting opinions, one may act in accordance with either view. After each talmudic objection to an opinion without subsequent decision, one may [likewise] adopt either that opinion or the tenor of the objection . . . Every *tequ* [a query officially left unanswered] ought to be decided in the more rigid vein if it relates to ritual prohibitions, and more liberally if it concerns monetary matters. Similarly, if the same rule

is stated in two conflicting versions, one must follow the more rigid line in cases of biblical law and take a more lenient view with respect to a rabbinic regulation.

8 Collated and edited by Aaron Hyman (London, 1910); A. Spanier, *Die Toseftaperiode in der tannaitischen Literatur* (Berlin, 1936) pp. 5ff.

9 Shulvass, op. cit., pp. 469–70.

10 Edited by R. J. L. Ha'Cohen Maimon under the title *Yehuse Tannaim Ve'Amoraim* (Jerusalem, 1963); see also E. E. Urbach, *Baalei Ha'Tosafot* (Jerusalem, 1955) pp. 307ff; Shulvass, op. cit., pp. 468–71; and A. A. Neuman, op. cit., pp. 255ff. Other examples of this historical genre given by Zunz (op. cit., p. 2) include the works of Menahem b. Solomon Meiri (Provence, 1249–1316) and of Isaac b. Jacob Lattes (Provence, fourteenth century).

11 *Mishneh Torah*, Book I: Knowledge, ch. 1; *Guide of the Perplexed*, III, 29. See also S. W. Baron, *History and Jewish Historians* (Philadelphia, 1968) pp. 116ff.

12 Some of the reasons for this difference are examined in G. D. Cohen, 'Messianic Postures of Ashkenazim and Sephardim', Leo Baeck Memorial Lecture 9 (New York, 1967).

13 *Seder Eliyahu Rabbah*, ed. Friedman, ch. 20.

14 *Torat Ha'Shem Temima*, ed. A. Jellinek (Leipzig, 1853) pp. 30ff; see also Nahmanides' commentary to Genesis II, 3; and Hayyim Bazak, 'Ma'aseh Avoth Siman le'banim be'Perush Ha'Ramban', *Ha'Ma'ayan*, xv, 3 (1975) 11–19.

15 Exodus XVII, 9, Nahmanides, ad. loc. Note Baron's remarks concerning the historical outlook of medieval Jewry:

It viewed all happenings under the aspect of long-range historic implications, in which a generation, even a century, mattered little because the basic lines of evolution had long been predicted by the ancient prophets. If asked, most medieval Jews would unhesitatingly have asserted that they were more apt to detect the true meaning of contemporary events by restudying the ancient prophetic messages than by pondering over minute details of these events themselves. For this reason the constant immersion in the words of Scripture . . . appeared to the majority as far more useful a pursuit for the understanding of their own time than the ascertainment of specific facts of their contemporary experience. Bible and tradition thus became the main guideposts for historical understanding, as they were important vehicles of the historical evolution itself. (op. cit., VI, p. 234.)

16 Ed. A. Poznanski, revised and introduced by Julius Guttmann (Berlin, 1924) p. 1; for b. Hiyya's other works and interests see L. Stitskin, *Judaism as a Philosophy* (New York, 1960) and *The Meditation of the Sad Soul*, ed. and trans. G. Wigoder (London, 1969).

17 *Megilat Ha'Megaleh*, p. 21; see also p. 84.

18 But he did not rate this very highly – cf. ibid., p. 11.

19 See above p. 7.

20 Op. cit., p. 20. See also *T.B. Sanhedrin*, 97a. The exegesis of Genesis in this way was hitherto all but unknown in Jewish tradition and it has been conjectured by Guttman (introduction, p. xiii) that it came to b. Hiyya from Isidore of Seville, though the former had of course to change the meaning to suit Jewish, as against Christian, purposes. The exegesis attains its classic expression in St Augustine's *City of God*. For a recent exposition cf. R. W. Southern, 'Aspects of the European tradition of historical writing : 2. Hugh of St. Victor and the idea of historical development', *Transactions of the Royal Historical Society*, 5th series, vol. xxi (1971) 159ff.

21 *Megilat Ha'megaleh*, p. 36.

22 See I. Baer, 'Eine jüdische Messiasprophetie auf das Jahr 1186 und der dritte Kreuzzug' and II, 'Messianische Bewegungen um 1186' (*M.G.W.J.*, Hefte 3/4, 5/6, 1926). Chazan (op. cit., pp. 123ff), in arguing that R. Ephraim's martyrology was written in the late 1170s, notes also that it is informed by 'a strong sense of impending confrontation between the great power blocs of Christendom and Islam'.

23 *Megilat Ha'Megaleh*, p. 144.

24 Ibid., pp. 146ff.

25 Critical edition and translation, G. D. Cohen (London, 1969).

26 Cf. Ben-Sasson, op. cit., pp. 36ff.

27 I. Elbogen, *Abraham Ibn Daud als Geschichtsschreiber, Festschrift für Jakob Guttman* (Leipzig, 1915) p. 187.

28 *Sefer Ha'Qabbalah* (The Book of Tradition), prologue. I have followed the translation of G. D. Cohen.

29 Page 66 (Hebrew text).

30 G. D. Cohen, op. cit., p. 288; see also I. Baer, *Toldoth Ha'Yehudim bi'Sefarad Ha'Notzrit*, 2nd ed., vol. i (Tel Aviv, 1965) pp. 38–9, and G. D. Cohen's *Messianic Postures*, pp. 19ff.

31 Op. cit., p. 66.

32 Ibid., p. 6.

33 Ibid., p. 74. By 'Sadducees', Ibn Daud meant the Karaites.

34 Quoted G. D. Cohen, op. cit., p. 214.

E*

35 See above, pp. 23ff.
36 Acknowledgement for this analysis is gratefully made to the work of G. D. Cohen in his edition of Ibn Daud's work, particularly his chapter 'The Four Empires and Jewish History', op. cit., pp. 223–62.
37 Philippe Wolff, 'The 1391 Pogrom in Spain – Social Crisis or not?', *Past and Present*, no. 50 (Feb 1971).
38 The quincentenary of Abrabanel's birth produced a number of studies of his career, writings, etc : Erwin I. J. Rosenthal, 'Don Isaac Abrabanel : Financier, Statesman and Scholar', *Bulletin of the John Rylands Library* (Manchester, 1937) now reprinted in *Studia Semitica*, I (Cambridge University Press, 1971); I. Baer, 'Don Yitzhak Abrabanel Ve'Yahso el Baiyot Ha'Historiya Ve'Ha'Medina' and M. Segal, 'R. Yitzhak Abrabanel b'Tor Parshan Ha'Mikrah', both *Tarbitz*, VIII, nos. 3–4 (Jerusalem, 1937); and Abraham Heschel, *Don Yizchak Abrabanel* (Berlin, 1937).
39 This is very largely based on the interpretation of the book of Daniel. For the precise mode of calculation see J. Sarachek, *The Doctrine of the Messiah in Medieval Jewish Literature*, 2nd ed. (New York, 1968), pp. 244ff.; see also Segal, op. cit., p. 276, and Jakob Guttmann, *Die religionsphilosophischen Lehren des Isaak Abravanel* (Breslau, 1916) pp. 99–100, n. 2.
40 B. Netanyahu, *Don Isaac Abrabanel* (Philadelphia, 1968) pp. 245ff; J. Rohr, 'Die Prophetie im letzten Jahrhundert vor der Reformation als Geschichtsquelle und Geschichtsfaktor', *Historisches Jahrbuch der Görresgesellschaft*, XIX, (Munich, 1898) pp. 29–56, 447–66.
41 Netanyahu, op. cit., pp. 200ff.
42 *Ma'ayenei Ha'Yeshuah* (Stettin, 1860) introduction, p. 3b.
43 *Ateret Zekenim* (Warsaw, 1894) p. 34. Abrabanel's attitude to astrology is not clear. For a discussion cf. E. Shmueli, *Don Yitzchak Abrabanel ve'Gerush Sepharad* (Jerusalem, 1963) pp. 127ff. In any case it is clear that Israel's good deeds could avert an unfavourable planetary conjunction (p. 132); see also Sarachek, op. cit., p. 297, and Guttman, op. cit., pp. 51ff.
44 Quoted *Ateret Zekenim*, p. 106. Abrabanel replaces 'Jacob' by 'Israel'.
45 Rosenthal, op. cit., p. 49 (473).
46 *Ateret Zekenim*, p. 106.
47 I. Baer, in *Tarbitz*, VIII, 3–4 (1937) 257.
48 *Mashmia Yeshuah* (Offenbach, 1767 p. 51a.
49 *Ma'ayenei Ha'Yeshuah*, p. 17b.

50 *Yeshuot Meshiho*, (Königsberg, 1861) pp. 26a–b (2nd ed. Jerusalem, 1967); see also Netanyahu, op. cit., pp. 206–7.
51 *Yeshuot Meshiho*, pp. 33b ff.
52 See Leo Strauss's remarks in *Isaac Abrabanel*, ed. Trend-Loewe (Cambridge, 1937) pp. 108–9.
53 *Ma'ayenei Ha'Yeshuah*, p. 48a.
54 For the details see Netanyahu, op. cit., pp. 211ff, and Segal, op. cit., pp. 275–6.
55 *Yeshuot Meshiho*, pp. 15a, 10a–b.
56 Ibid.
57 *Ma'ayenei Ha'Yeshuah*, p. 50b.
58 See Guttmann's introduction, *Megilat Ha'Megaleh*, pp. xxvi–xxvii; *Ma'ayenei Ha'Yeshuah*, p. 48a.
59 *Yeshuot Meshiho*, p. 35b.
60 Ibid., p. 34b ff.
61 See Netanyahu, op. cit., pp. 228ff.
62 *Mashmia*, p. 77b.

Chapter 4

1 Quoted H. H. Ben-Sasson, *Galut u'Geulah b'eynav shel dor Golé Sepharad*, Baer Jubilee volume (Jerusalem, 1960) p. 225, and the same author's 'The Reformation in Contemporary Jewish Eyes', *Proceedings of Israel Academy of Sciences and Humanities*, iv, no. 12 (Jerusalem, 1970) 22ff. There was in fact no uniform Jewish view of Luther. Josel of Rosheim, for example, recognised by Charles V as 'the Commander of Jewry' in the Holy Roman Empire, gave his support to Pope and Emperor (cf. S. Stern, 'Josel of Rosheim', *JPSA*, 1965).
2 *Zemach David* (Lemberg, 1847) p. 112a.
3 G. Scholem, *Major Trends in Jewish Mysticism*, p. 284.
4 *Gevuroth Ha'Shem*, new ed. (London, 1971) first preface, p. 3.
5 *Netzah Israel*, new ed. (London, 1960) ch. 1, p. 9.
6 *Gevuroth Ha'Shem*, ch. lxvii, p. 311; see also A. Kariv (ed.), *Kitve Maharal mi'Prag* (Jerusalem, 1972) vol. 1, introduction, p. 32.
7 *Gevuroth Ha'Shem*, ch. iii, p. 27.
8 *Tifereth Israel* (Jerusalem, ed; 1970) ch. lxiv, p. 195; see also *Or Hadash* (Jerusalem, 1944) p. 1a and *Netivot Olam, Netiv Ha'Tseniut* (Warsaw, 1844) ch. 3.
9 *Or Hadash*, p. 1b.
10 *Be'er Ha'Golah* (Jerusalem ed., 1971) ch. v, p. 148.
11 *Netzah Israel*, ch. ix, pp. 70–1.
12 See e.g. Julius Voos, 'David Reuveni und Salomo Molcho', in-

augural dissertation (Bonn, 1933); and G. Scholem, *Sabbatai Sevi, The Mystical Messiah 1626–1676* (London, 1973).

13 A. Klempt, *Die Säkularisierung der universalhistorischen Auffassung im 16 und 17 Jahrhundert* (Göttingen, 1960), p.13.
14 Ibid., pp. 43, 64ff.
15 See below pp. 41, 48 and H. H. Ben-Sasson, 'Musagim u'metziut ba'historiya ha'yehudit b'shilhe ymei ha'beinayim', *Tarbitz*, xxix (1959–60) 305–6.
16 M. Shulvass, *Hayyei Ha'Yehudim B'Italiya Bi'Tkufat Ha'Renaissance* (New York, 1955) pp. 286ff.
17 See Isaac Baer, *Galut* (Berlin, 1936) pp. 64ff and the same author's introduction to *Shevet Yehuda*, ed. A. Schochat (repr. Jerusalem, 1947).
18 See I. Loeb, 'Josef Ha'Cohen et les chroniqueurs juifs', *Revue des Etudes Juives*, xxiv (Paris, 1892) pp. 1–29.
19 *Shevet Yehuda*, no. 7.
20 Ibid., no. 24; cf. also no. 44 and Neuman, op. cit., pp. 261ff.
21 Ibid., no. 7.
22 Ibid., no. 63.
23 *Zemach David*, introduction, p. 2b.
24 Ed. H. Filipowski (Edinburgh, 1857); first published Constantinople, 1566.
25 Preface, p.1.
26 See Maimonides' introduction to his commentary on the Mishnah where he states, after enumerating the rabbis quoted, 'I did not trouble myself to mention their names in accordance with the sequence of their times'.
27 Op. cit., p. 2.
28 Ibid., pp. 2–3.
29 Ibid., p. 216.
30 Ibid., pp. 217–23.
31 Ibid., p. 11.
32 Ibid., p. 231.
33 Ibid., pp. 232ff.
34 *Shalshelet Ha'Kabbalah* (Warsaw ed., 1877) pp. 3–4.
35 Ibid., p. 4.
36 Ibn Yahya, op. cit., pp. 97–124, 124–60.
37 A. Gottesdiener, 'Ha'Ari she b'Hochmei Prag', *Azkarah le Ha'Rav Kuk*, ed. J. L. Fischmann, iv (Jerusalem, 1937) p. 343.
38 Quoted H. H. Ben-Sasson, 'Jews and Christian Sectarians', *Viator*, 4 (1973) 374–5; see also M. Breuer, 'Kavim l'demuto shel R. David Gans', *Annual of the University of Bar Ilan*, xi

(1973) 104; and Fynes Moryson, *Shakespeare's Europe*, ed. Charles Hughes (repr. New York, 1967) pp. 275, 489; cf. also A. Néher, *David Gans* (Paris, 1974) pt. i. This is the most recent study of Gans' life and work in the context of his time.

39 Quoted Breuer, op. cit., p. 102.

40 J. Kohn, *Soziologische Einführungsskizze in die Geschichts-schreibung des Judentums in der Çeskoslovakischen Republik* (Jahrbuch der Gesellschaft für die Geschichte der Juden in der Çeskoslovakischen Republik, ii, 1930, pp. 10ff).

41 Weinryb, op. cit., pp. 943–4.

42 See below, pp. 47–8ff.

43 Op. cit., p. 2a.

44 Ibid., p. 2b.

45 Gans, op. cit., p. 36b.

46 Ibid., pp. 43b ff.

47 Ibid., p. 2a. (In the extract quoted here the Emperor is referred to as Leopold. This is evidently the result of the up-dating undertaken by the editor of the 1847 edition.) This latter omits the last part of the quotation which is present however in the Hominer reprint (Jerusalem, 1966) p. 3.

48 Ibid., p. 62a; see also Jirina Sedinova, 'Non-Jewish Sources in "The Chronicle" by David Gans' and 'Czech history as reflected in the historical work by David Gans', *Judaica Bohemiae*, viii, nos. 1 and 2 (Prague, 1972).

49 *Shulhan Arukh, Orech Hayim*, 307, 16.

50 Gans, op. cit., p. 62a.

51 Ibid., p. 61b.

52 Ibid.

53 Ibid.

54 Ibid., p. 86a.

55 Ibid., p. 112b.

56 Ibid., pp. 62a–63a. The reference to Isserlis is to his glosses on the geometrical work *Yessod Olam*, by the fourteenth century astronomer of Toledo, Isaac b. Joseph Israeli. Isserlis wrote: 'I have noted the renowned non-Jewish philosophers divided according to their names and times so that we may know the sequence of the generations that have passed until today for from the sages of the Gentiles we may find evidence for our own.' (See A. Siev, *Rabbi Moses Isserlis*, New York, 1972, pp. 174–5.)

57 Gans, op. cit., p. 65a; see also Ben-Sasson, *Musagim u'metziut*, p. 306.

58 M. Breuer, 'Magamotav shel Zemach David', *Ha'Ma'ayan*, v,

no. 2 (1965) 15–27 is a superb analysis of these points. It may also be that the inclination not to disturb relations with the Gentile world led Gans to omit from Part I of his chronicle any reference to the Prague mob's plundering of the ghetto during a fire in 1559 and the confiscation of Hebrew books instigated by an apostate Jew, Yehuda of Udine (see S. Steinherz, 'Sage und Geschichte', *Jahrbuch der Gesellschaft für die Geschichte der Juden in der C-S Republik*, IX (1938) 178ff).

59 Hominer ed., p. 183.

60 M. A. Shulvass, *Hayye Ha'Yehudim B'Italiya Bi'Tkufat Ha' Renaissance* (New York, 1955) esp. chs 6–8.

61 See above, pp. 41, 48.

62 See S. W. Baron, 'Azariah dei Rossi's Historical Method', *History and Jewish Historians* (Philadelphia, 1964) 205–39.

63 A. Néher, *Le Puits de l'Exil* (Paris, 1966) pp. 100–1.

64 *Me'or Eynayim, Imrei Bina*, ed. D. Cassel (Vilna, 1866) ch. XLIII, p. 370.

65 Ibid., chs XLff.

66 Ibid., ch. I, p. 80. The references to Cicero are to Bk 1, para. 3 of *Rhetorica ad Herennium* – in modern editions ch. VIII, para. 12; Bk 5 of letters to various friends, letter 13 to Lucceius.

67 Ibid., ch. XIV, p. 197.

68 Ibid., ch. XII, p. 189.

69 Ibid., ch. XXXVIII, pp. 269–70.

70 Ibid., ch. XII, p. 182.

71 Ibid., ch. XIV, p. 196.

72 Quoted *Imrei Bina*, ch. XXVII, p. 268. Rossi's abbreviated reference has been given in full.

73 Ibid., pp. 154, 268, 277.

74 Ibid., p. 205.

75 For all above see ibid., ch. XVI, pp. 214–19. There is an English translation of the salient portions of this chapter in M. A. Meyer (ed.), *Ideas of Jewish History* (New York, 1974) pp. 117ff.

76 *Imrei Bina*, ch. XXIII, p. 253.

77 Ibid., ch. XXVII, pp. 264ff.

78 Y. L. Zunz, *Toldoth R. Azariah min Ha'Edumın, Matzref la' Kessef*, ed. Isaac Ben-Yaakov, III (Vilna, 1865) p. 5 (Hebrew pagination).

79 Kaufmann, op. cit. III, pp. 83–95; see also S. Bernfeld, *Bnei Aliya* (Tel Aviv, 1931) p. 150.

80 Gans, op. cit., pp. 2a, 6a, 18a, 19a, 61b, 61b–62a, 68a. For the use made by Ibn Yahya, see Shulvass, op. cit., p. 294.

81 See Gottesdiener, op. cit., p. 291 and Maharal, *Gevuroth Ha'Shem*, second preface, p. 8.
82 *Be'er Ha'Golah*, ch. vi, p. 141.
83 Ibid., p. 134; cf. also pp. 126–7.
84 See, for example, J. Elbaum, 'R. Judah Loew of Prague and his Attitude to the Aggadah', *Scripta Hierosolymitana*, xxii (1971) pp. 28–47.
85 *Be'er Ha'Golah*, ch. vi, p. 127.
86 *Imrei Bina*, ch. xiv, p. 196.
87 *Be'er Ha'Golah*, ch. vi, p. 135.
88 *Gevuroth Ha'Shem*, second preface, p. 7.
89 *Be'er Ha'Golah*, ch. vi, p. 106.
90 See Néher, op. cit., pp. 98–116.
91 *Be'er Ha'Golah*, pp. 112, 131.
92 Ibid., ch. vi, pp. 137–9.
93 Zunz, op. cit., pp. 7ff (Heb.).
94 Ibid., p. 4 (Heb.).

Chapter 5

1 Y. Halperin, introduction to *Seder Ha'Dorot* (repr. Jerusalem, 1970) pp. 3–5.
2 *Megilat Sefer*, ed. D. Cahana (Warsaw, 1896) pp. 96–8.
3 Israel Rabin, 'Stoff und Idee in der jüdischen Geschichtsschreibung', in *Dubnow Festschrift*, ed. Elbogen, Meisl, Wischnitzer (Berlin, 1930) p. 51; for Baer see his 'Le'Berur ha'Matzav shel ha'limudim ha'historiim etzlenu', *Sefer Magnes* (Jerusalem, 1938). Baer writes: 'the influence of the *Torah* and the prophets and the pressure of a hard destiny' transformed a realistic historical approach into a religious system which conditioned the activity and thought of Israel until the eighteenth century. But the religious relationship to historical experience 'is absolutely opposed to the basic aspirations of modern historiography' (p. 31).
4 See Elon, op. cit., pp. 65ff and the literature cited there.
5 See also A. Altmann, *Moses Mendelssohn* (London, 1973) pp. 455ff and 472ff.
6 See the material quoted from R. Isaiah Hurewitz and others in H. H. Ben-Sasson, *Hagut Ve'Hanhaga* (Jerusalem, 1959) pp. 91, 124.
7 'Civil Disabilities of the Jews', *Edinburgh Review* (1831).
8 B. Mevorah (ed.), *Napoleon u'tekufato* (Jerusalem, 1968) pp. 173ff, 186ff; Israel Berger, *Esser Tsahtsahot* (Piotrkow, 1910) p. 87.

9 *Publications of the American Jewish Historical Society*, no. 27, II (1920) 140–1.

10 See e.g. F. Kobler, *The Vision Was There* (London, 1956) pp. 42ff, and M. Vereté, 'The Restoration of the Jews in English Protestant Thought 1790–1840', *Middle Eastern Studies* (Jan. 1972).

11 See B. Mevorah, 'The Problem of the Messiah in the Emancipation and Reform Controversies 1781–1819', unpublished Ph.D. thesis (Jerusalem, 1966).

12 For a convenient guide to views expressed at these conferences see Isaac Barzilay, *Shlomo Yehudah Rapaport* (Israel, 1969) pp. 115ff.

13 *Religion der Vernunft aus den Quellen des Judentums* (Leipzig, 1919) p. 293; see also Simon Kaplan, *Das Geschichtsproblem in der Philosophie Hermann Cohens* (Berlin, 1930) pp. 96ff.

14 *Religion der Vernunft*, p. 426.

15 M. D. Herr, 'Role of the Halacha in the Shaping of Jewish History', *Contemporary Thinking in Israel*, I (Jerusalem, 1973) pp. 42ff.

16 *Gesammelte Schriften*, V. Briefe, ed. G. B. Mendelssohn (Leipzig, 1844) 16 Feb 1765, p. 342. But there were exceptions, e.g. Mendelssohn found Hume's *History of England* 'incomparable' and particularly admired Hume's ability to 'develop characters and events' (ibid., 2 Nov 1762, p. 268).

17 For Aristotle, see above, p. 15: for Descartes, *Discours de la Méthode*, pt 1.

18 See E. Cassirer, *Die Idee der Religion bei Lessing und Mendelssohn*, Festgabe zum zehnjährigen Bestehen der Akademie für die Wissenschaft des Judentums 1919–1929 (Berlin, 1929) p. 32; S. Bernfeld, *Mendelssohns Wirken im Judentum, Mendelssohn–zur 200-jährigen Wiederkehr seines Geburtstages, Encyclopaedia Judaica* (Berlin, 1929) pp. 69ff.

19 See above, p. 12.

20 *Gesammelte Schriften*, v, 20 July 1764, p. 325; for Abbt's letter to Mendelssohn see p. 321.

21 Ibid., 22 July 1766, p. 368. The perplexities of Mendelssohn were of course intensified and multiplied in the following generation of German Jews to whom there existed a real possibility of entering German society – but on what terms? (See Rosenthal, op. cit., pp. 52ff and Leo Baeck, *Aus drei Jahrtausenden*, Tübingen, 1958, p. 32.)

22 Mendelssohn, op. cit.

23 See Mendelssohn's *Jerusalem*, ch. 2.
24 Maimon, op. cit., pp. 134–5.
25 *Divrei Shalom Ve'Emeth* (Words of Peace and Truth), Letter 1, ch. 4.
26 For a short account of these developments see N. N. Glatzer, 'The Beginnings of Modern Jewish Studies', in A. Altmann (ed.), *Studies in Nineteenth-Century Jewish Intellectual History* (Cambridge, Mass., 1964) pp. 27–45; I. Barzilay, op. cit., pp. 49ff; B.-Z. Katz, *Rabbanut, Hasidut, Haskala* (Jerusalem, 1956, 1958) I, pp. 230ff, II, pp. 204ff. Significantly, Radday writes: 'Modern historiography written by Jews began as late as the Napoleonic era with papers published in the Hebrew periodical *Sulamit* by Solomon Loewysohn [*sic*] (1789–1822).' ('Does Archaeology Contribute to a Better Understanding of Scripture?' *Dispersion and Unity*, 19/20 (1973) 156.) See also R. Michael, 'Trumat ktav-ha'et "Shulamit" la'historiografiya ha'yehudit ha'hadasha', *Zion*, XXXIX, nos. 1–2 (1974).
27 Quoted Glatzer, op. cit., p. 40; see also Georg Herlitz, 'Three Jewish Historians', *Yearbook of the Leo Baeck Institute*, IX (London, 1964), 71–6; Barzilay, op. cit., pp. 15–16; and M. Meyer, 'Where Does Modern Jewish History Begin?' *Judaism*, XXIV, 3 (1975) 330.
28 H. G. Reissner, 'Rebellious Dilemma', *Year Book of Leo Baeck Institute*, II (London, 1957) 179–93; Michael A. Meyer, 'Jewish Religious Reform and Wissenschaft des Judentums', ibid., XVI (1971) 19–41.
29 Ibid., II (1957) 194ff.
30 M. Meyer, *Origins of the Modern Jew* (Detroit, 1967) pp. 158ff; F. Bamberger, 'Zunz's Conception of History', *Proceedings of the American Academy for Jewish Research*, XI (1941) pp. 11ff.
31 N. Glatzer, 'Klalim b'tfisat-ha'historiya shel Zunz', *Zion*, XXI (1961) 208–14.
32 Kurt Wilhelm, 'Zur Einführung in die Wissenschaft des Judentums', *Wissenschaft des Judentums im deutschen Sprachbereich*, I (Tübingen, 1966) pp. 5–6.
33 *Gesammelte Schriften*, I, p. 4.
34 Ibid., p. 57.
35 Ibid., p. 65.
36 *Leviticus Rabbah* (Behukkotai), XXXV, 7.
37 Cf. Bamberger, op. cit., p. 8.
38 Note Acton's remarks in his Inaugural Lecture of 1894: 'Philosophers claim that as early as 1804 they began to bow the metaphysical neck beneath the historical yoke. They taught

that philosophy is only the amended sum of all philosophies, that systems pass with the age whose impress they bear, that the problem is to focus the rays of wandering but extant truth, and that history is the source of philosophy, if not quite a substitute for it' (*Essays on Freedom and Power*, ed. G. Himmelfarb, Boston, 1948, p. 23); see also E. Fackenheim, *Metaphysics and Historicity* (Milwaukee, 1961) p. 4.

39 *Igrot Shadal*, pt vii, ed. Graeber (Cracow, 1884) p. 1367.

40 In 1840, Luzzatto wrote to Jost in Frankfurt: 'When, dear German scholars, when will the Lord open your eyes? And when will you not see that you are being drawn after the crowd, and letting your national pride be extinguished and the tongue of our fathers be forgotten from the lips of our sons, and Atticism grow daily in our midst, and how long will you allow your brethren to imagine a picture of perfection such as lay only in approximation to their neighbours, to become important in their eyes . . . and that the good of our people does not depend on emancipation but on the love of man for his brother . . . this is our good and this is dwindling and vanishing in the shadow of emancipation . . .' (ibid., v, p. 660); cf. also D. Rudavsky, 'S. D. Luzzatto and Neo-Orthodoxy', *Tradition*, vii, no. 3 (1965) 21–42.

41 S. R. Hirsch, *Gesammelte Schriften*, i, p. 131. I have used the translation, slightly adapted, of Dr I. Grunfeld, *Judaism Eternal* (London, 1956), i, pp. 133–5. Baeck (op. cit., p. 33) makes precisely the same attack: 'History began to mean more than the content'.

Chapter 6

1 J. Neusner, 'Review Essay – Ideas of Jewish History', *History and Theory*, xiv, no. 2 (1975) 220.

2 N. Rotenstreich, 'Hegel's Image of Judaism', *Jewish Social Studies*, xv, 1 (Jan 1953) 33–52.

3 *Geschichte der Juden*, xi, p. 483.

4 See e.g. P. Lachover, *Al Gvul Ha'Yashan Ve'He'Hadash* (Jerusalem, 1951) p. 263.

5 All references here are to *Kitve Rabbi Nahman Krochmal*, ed. S. Rawidowicz (London, 1961), hereafter cited as *Kitve*.

6 Lachover, op. cit., p. 176.

7 *Kitve*, pp. 202, 209.

8 S. Rawidowicz, 'Ranak b'tor hoker u'mvaker', *Ha'Shiloach*, xlii, 2 (1924) 170.

9   From Krochmal's introduction to *Moreh Nevuche Ha'Zman*, p. 5; cf. also pp. 149 and 211.

10 See also S. Rawidowicz, 'Nahman Krochmal als Historiker', *Dubnow Festschrift* (Berlin, 1930) p. 58.

11 Rawidowicz, op. cit., *Ha'Shiloach*, xlii, no. 3 (1924) pp. 253–4.

12 *Kitve*, p. 24–7.

13 P. Bloch, *Heinrich Graetz, A Memoir* (London, 1898) pp. 16ff; see also H. Liebeschütz, *Das Judentum im deutschen Geschichtsbild von Hegel bis Max Weber* (Tübingen, 1967) pp. 139ff. Graetz spoke appreciatively of Braniss in his *Konstruktion*, p. 94.

14 W. Boehlich (ed.), *Der Berliner Antisemitismusstreit* (Frankfurt a.M., 1965); H. Liebeschütz, 'Treitschke und Mommsen', *Leo Baeck Year Book*, vii (1962) 153–82.

15 S. W. Baron, *History and Jewish Historians* (Philadelphia, 1964) 268; R. Michael, 'Zvi Graetz – Toldoth Hayav', in S. Ettinger (ed.), *Graetz, Darkhe Ha'Historiya Ha'Yehudit* (Jerusalem, 1969) p. 50.

16 H. Cohen, *Jüdische Schriften*, ii (Berlin, 1924) pp. 85–6. This was written in 1880.

17 Ibid., pp. 418ff, and iii, pp. 203–12. For a contemporary attempt to relieve German Jewry of responsibility for Graetz's views see E. Schreiber, *Graetzens Geschichtsbauerei* (Berlin, 1881).

18 There is a most sensitive and subtle exposition of this conflict in Erwin I. J. Rosenthal, 'Hermann Cohen and Heinrich Graetz', *S. W. Baron Jubilee Volume*, ii (Jerusalem, 1974) pp. 725–43.

19 Dubnow, *Weltgeschichte*, x, p. 31.

20 *Geschichte*, iv, introduction, p. 1.

21 Ibid., pp. 4–5; cf. also introduction to v.

22 *Kitve*, p. 286.

23 Ibid., p. 296. For further discussion of this point see P. Lachover, 'Nigleh V'Nistar B'Mishnato shel Ranak', op. cit., pp. 212–13; and S. Schwarzschild, 'Two Modern Jewish Philosophers of History, Nahman Krochmal and Hermann Cohen', unpublished Ph.D thesis, Hebrew Union College (Cincinnati, 1955) pp. 15–17.

24 *Kitve*, p. 59.

25 *Kitve*, p. 71. Why 'the spirit' should be 'the main thing' is examined below, p. 75.

26 *Kitve*, pp. 13, 209. For further discussion of this point see Rawidowicz, *Mevo*, pp. 138–9, and Schwarzschild, op. cit., pp. 16–17.

27   *Kitve*, p. 88.
28   See the examples cited by Rawidowicz, *Mevo*, pp. 106, 173;
     also the same author's *Iyunim*, II (Jerusalem, 1971) p. 242.
     Others who have pointed, with varying degrees of emphasis,
     to an apparent connection between Vico and Krochmal are
     B. Gross, *Le messianisme Juif* p. 79; Schwarzschild, op. cit.,
     p. 32. There has been much discussion of the sources of Kroch-
     mal's inspiration. Formerly this was conducted primarily with-
     in the framework of the question : was he a Hegelian or not?
     (cf. J. L. Landau, *Nachman Krochmal – ein Hegelianer* (Ber-
     lin, 1904) and S. Rawidowicz, 'War Nachman Krochmal
     Hegelianer?' *Hebrew Union College Annual* (Cincinnati, 1928)
     vi. In more recent years, the discussion has been deepened in
     such a way as strongly to suggest the presence of neo-Platonic
     and gnostic elements with reminiscences of Philo, Yehuda
     Halevi, Nahmanides and Abraham Ibn Ezra (cf. Schwarzschild,
     op. cit., pp. 58–75, and Lachover, op. cit., pp. 173–263).
29   *Kitve*, pp. 34–5.
30   Ibid., p. 35.
31   Ibid., pp. 36–7.
32   Ibid.
33   See eg. Abraham Katsh, 'Nachman Krochmal and the German
     Idealists', *Jewish Social Studies*, VIII (1946) 87–102.
34   *Kitve*, p. 35.
35   Ibid., p. 37; cf. also *Nahum*, III, 8.
36   Quoted *Kitve*, p. 37.
37   For references see L. Ginzberg, *Legends of the Jews*, III, p. 25;
     VI, p. 8 n. 41, p. 391 n. 25.
38   *Kitve*, pp. 37–8.
39   Ibid., p. 38.
40   Ibid., pp. 38–9.
41   Ibid., p. 42.
42   Ibid., p. 39. For the light that the subjective factor casts on
     the idea of revelation see Gross, op. cit., p. 80, n. 25.
43   *Kitve*, p. 36.
44   Whereas Vico appears to have made a basic distinction. He
     wrote in his Autobiography (ed. and trans. Fisch and Bergin,
     New York, 1963, pp. 171–2) : 'He [i.e. Vico] always takes
     account of the essential differences between the Hebrews and
     Gentiles. The former from the beginning arose and stood stead-
     fast on the practices of an eternal justice. The pagan nations,
     however, by the sole guidance of divine providence, underwent
     with constant uniformity the successive variations of three kinds

of laws corresponding to the three ages and languages of the Egyptians'.

45 *Haggai*, I, 13; II, 5, quoted *Kitve*, p. 52; cf. also the Talmudic passage referred to below, p. 79.

46 N. Rotenstreich, *Tradition and Reality* (New York, 1972) pp. 46–7, makes a cogent contrast; see also the same author's 'T'fisto Ha'Historit shel Ranak', *Zion*, VII (1942) 46–7 for the differences between Krochmal's cycles and those of Vico. The *Sefer Ha'Temunah*, a cabalistic work of the thirteenth century, puts forward a theory of cosmic cycles, each of seven thousand years' duration, after each of which the world again arises from chaos. In the fiftieth millenium, after seven such cycles, the world returns to nothingness in preparation for a new *creatio ex nihilo*.

47 *Kitve*, pp. 40–9.

48 Ibid., p. 51.

49 Ibid., p. 112.

50 Ibid., pp. 40–1.

51 Cf. Rawidowicz, *Mevo*, p. 124, and J. Taubes, 'Krochmal and Modern Historicism', *Judaism*, XII, no. 2, p. 159.

52 *Kitve*, p. 273.

53 *Geschichte*, I (Leipzig, 1874 ed.) pp. XXXIV–XXXV, introduction. Graetz only mentions the first two periods which are as follows : 'from the crystallization of the Israelite family groups into a people and entry into Canaan until the emergence of the Kingdom forms the first epoch, that of growth. The second epoch, that of efflorescence, is formed by the rule of David and Solomon who raised the Israelite people to a state of the first magnitude. The blossoming was short, and gradual decline in strength followed and finally the collapse of the people. But it rose again, gradually grew under the rule of Persia and Greece, again developed a resplendent flowering under the Maccabees, only to collapse once again through the Romans'.

54 *Konstruktion*, pp. 8–9.

55 Ibid., p. 9.

56 Ibid, pp. 11ff. This relationship has been ascribed to the influence of Steinheim, cf. H. Cohen, op. cit., III, p. 204.

57 *Konstruktion*, pp. 15–18. Graetz's traditional roots are all the more evident when contrasted to the liberal innovation of Geiger for whom Judaism 'owed its enduring nature to its independence from the political base' *(von dem politischen Bestande)* (A. Geiger, *Nachgelassene Schriften*, II, ed. L. Geiger, Berlin, 1875, p. 62). Graetz's antipathy to the reform and liberal

trends in nineteenth-century Judaism is superbly expounded in
I. Schorsch (ed. and trans.), *Heinrich Graetz – The Structure
of Jewish History and other essays* (New York, 1975) introduction.

58   *Konstruktion*, pp. 18–20.
59   Ibid., p. 96.
60   He later wrote : 'The real historical process only begins with
the Exodus' (*Geschichte*, I, p. xii, introduction).
61   Ibid., pp. 22–32.
62   Ibid., p. 36.
63   Ibid., pp. 38–40.
64   Ibid., pp. 41–6.
65   Ibid., pp. 50ff.
66   Ibid., p. 88.
67   Ibid., pp. 52, 96. For further exposition of this point cf.
N. Rotenstreich, 'Nisyono shel Graetz ba'filosofiya shel ha'
historiya', *Zion*, VIII, no. 1 (1943) esp. pp. 56ff.
68   *Geschichte*, I, pp. 94–5. In the actual *Geschichte* of which
Volume XI (written some twenty years later) dealt with this
period, Graetz saw the Mendelssohnian era as the first period
of the fourth epoch of Jewish history and he entitled it 'the
time of growing self-consciousness'.
69   Ibid., p. 32.
70   See Schorsch, op. cit., pp. 55ff.
71   'Die Verjüngung des jüdischen Stammes', *Jahrbuch für
Israeliten*, n.s., vol. X, Vienna (1864) 25.
72   *Entwicklungsstadien des Messiasglaubens*, ibid., vol. XI, Vienna
(1865) 27ff. It seems likely that Graetz may have been influenced
by Hess. The two men met in 1862 and remained on friendly
terms until Hess's death in 1875. (See E. Silberner, *Moses Hess*
(Leiden, 1966) pp. 480ff and R. Michael, 'Graetz und Hess',
Year Book of the Leo Baeck Institute, IX (1964) 91ff.) Hess
wrote in his *Rom und Jerusalem* (Epilogue 3, Die Genetische
Weltanschauung, Leipzig, 1862) that in the same way as the
Greek genius had a special vocation for the creation of works
of art so did 'the Jewish genius have a special vocation for
creations of the knowledge of God' (see also the Ninth Letter).
The Hess–Graetz relationship in this respect is discussed in
Ettinger, op. cit., pp. 24–6.
73   *Briefwechsel einer englischen Dame über Judentum und Semitismus* (Stuttgart, 1883) pp. 9–12, 50, 56. It has been suggested
that Graetz's admiration for George Eliot's *Daniel Deronda*
(1876) led him to give an English context to this work, cast in

the form of correspondence between an uninstructed English-Jewish lady and an informed Jew (see Schorsch, op. cit., pp. 59–60).

74 *Historic Parallels in Jewish History*, a discourse delivered at the Anglo-Jewish Historical exhibition, 16 June 1887 (London, 1887) p. 12; cf. also '. . . Judaism is the source alike of humanity, of monotheism and of religious rationalism. It still has its function to play, its mission to fulfil, in bringing back these ideals to reality' ('The Significance of Judaism for Present and Future', *Jewish Quarterly Review* (Oct 1888) no. 1, p. 13).

75 See above, p. 78.

76 See *Kitve*, pp. 44, 50ff, 60.

77 Taubes, op. cit., p. 160.

78 I. Schorsch, 'The Philosophy of History of Nahman Krochmal', *Judaism*, x, no. 3 (1961) 237–45.

79 See above, p. 72.

80 See above, p. 84.

81 *Konstruktion*, p. 21.

Chapter 7

1 *Jewish History – An Essay in the Philosophy of History*, English trans. (London, 1903) pp. 21–4. This essay was first published in 1893 as the introduction to an abortive Russian translation of Graetz's history in an abridged form.

2 Quoted M. Wischnitzer, 'Ha'Adrikhal shel Ha'Historiografiya Ha'Yehudit', in *Sefer Dubnow*, ed. S. Rawidowicz (London, Jerusalem, 1954) p. 145.

3 See Paul Sofer, 'Sergei Bershadsky', *He'Avar*, xx (1973) esp. p. 66.

4 Quoted R. Mahler, 'Ha'kitot ve'ha'zramim ha'tarbutiim b'divrei ymei Yisrael l'shitat Dubnov', in Rawidowicz (ed.), op. cit., p. 117; see also S. Dubnowa-Erlikh, *Zhizn i Tvorchestvo S. M. Dubnova* (New York, 1950) pp. 37, 49, 219.

5 *Weltgeschichte*, i, p. 64.

6 Ibid., iii, pp. 306–13.

7 J. Meisl, 'Chaye Shimon Dubnov', in Rawidowicz (ed.), op. cit., p. 27–8; Dubnow, *Mein Leben*, ed. Hurwicz (Berlin, 1937) pp. 50ff.

8 Cf. Sh. Auerbach, 'Shimon Dubnovs Shtellung tzu Yiddish un Hebräisch', in A. Steinberg (ed.), *Simon Dubnow, the Man and His Work*, World Jewish Congress (Paris, 1963) pp. 162–4.

9 K. Pinson (ed.), *Nationalism and History. Essays on Old and New Judaism by S. Dubnow*, (Philadelphia, 1958) 141.

10 J. Lestchinsky, 'Ha'Otonomizm Ve'Ha'Mikhtavim al Ha' Yahadut Ha'Yeshana Ve'Ha'Hadasha', in Rawidowicz (ed.), op. cit., p. 180.

11 Pinson, op. cit., p. 368. In his own day Dubnow hoped to see Russian citizens of Jewish nationality (*Weltgeschichte*, VIII, p. 79).

12 Pinson, op. cit., pp. 86–7.

13 Ibid., p. 102. From which it also follows that a Jew emancipated in France could not consider himself a French national of the Jewish faith. 'No one can be counted a member of the French nationality unless he is born a Frenchman, unless he is a son or grandson of Gallic stock or of a related stock, or is so linked with the French for many generations that he has inherited all the qualities and characteristics that are the fruits of the historical development of the French nation.' (p. 102)

14 *Weltgeschichte*, VII, p. 475.

15 Pinson, op. cit., p. 93.

16 *Jewish History*, pp. 16–17.

17 A. Steinberg, 'Die weltanschaulichen Voraussetzungen der jüdischen Geschichtsschreibung', *Festschrift zu Dubnows 70tem Geburtstag*, ed. Meisl, Elbogen, Wischnitzer (Berlin, 1930) p. 40, n.l.

18 Elbogen, 'Von Graetz bis Dubnow', ibid., p. 7.

19 Ibid., p. 17.

20 *Weltgeschichte*, I, introduction, p. xiv.

21 Ibid., p. xv.

22 *Mein Leben*, pp. 50–1.

23 *Weltgeschichte*, I, pp. xiv–xv.

24 Pinson, op. cit., pp. 139, 231.

25 H. Graetz, *Geschichte*, v, introduction, pp. 7–8.

26 M. Davis, 'Jewry East and West – The Correspondence of I. Friedländer and S. Dubnow', *Yivo Annual*, IX (New York, 1954) p. 27.

27 S. Dubnow, *Pinkas Ha'Medina* (repr. Jerusalem, 1969) introduction, p. xi.

28 Lavrov wrote in his *Istoricheskie Pisma* (St Petersburg, 1906) p. 204: 'But can one really for a moment accept that the prophets of the time of the first fall of Jerusalem, the medieval cabalists, talmudists and translators of Averroes, and the contemporaries of Heine, Rothschild, Meyerbeer, Marx and Lassalle have all represented one and the same idea in history?'

29 Pinson, op. cit., pp. 76–81.

30 *Weltgeschichte*, x, p. 346.

31 Ahad Ha'am, *Igroth V, 1913–1919* (Jerusalem, Berlin, 1924) p. 247.

32 Ibid., IV, *1908–1912*, p. 100.

Chapter 8

1 'To be a Jew *means* to be in *Golus*' (Diaspora) : F. Rosenzweig, *Briefe*, no. 36 (Berlin, 1935) 398. Zionism is 'a diagnostician of genius but a very mediocre practitioner, recognized the evil but gave the wrong therapy' ('Bildung und kein Ende', *Kleinere Schriften* (Berlin, 1937) p. 86, hereafter cited as *K.S.*).

2 Cf. pp. 80ff above.

3 *Briefe*, no. 46, p. 55.

4 For the family background see the article by Rivka Horwitz, 'Judaism despite Christianity', *Judaism*, XXIV, no. 3 (1975).

5 M. Schwartz, 'Mkomo shel Franz Rosenzweig ba'filosofiya shel ha'Yahadut', introduction to Hebrew translation of *Der Stern der Erlösung* (Jerusalem, 1970) p. 15.

6 'Atheistische Theologie', *K.S.*, p. 282.

7 'Die Bauleute', ibid., p. 112. The orthodoxy of Samson Raphael Hirsch came off no better (ibid., p. 111). The flavour of Geiger's identification of liberal Judaism with the idea of progress can be gleaned from his periodisation of Jewish history : the revelation to the end of the Biblical period; the period of rabbinic tradition to the conclusion of the Babylonian Talmud; rigid legalism to the mid-eighteenth century; and, lastly, the period of liberation and criticism (A. Geiger, *Nachgelassene Schriften*, II, ed. L. Geiger, Berlin, 1875, pp. 61–63). For Rosenzweig's work as a hostile reaction to liberalism, cf. R. Horwitz, 'Tfisat Ha'Historiya Ha'Yehudit b'Mahashevet Rosenzweig', *Proceedings of the American Academy for Jewish Research* (New York, 1969) 10.

8 *Briefe*, no. 365, p. 476. This helps to explain Rosenzweig's admiration for Spengler (see *Briefe*, no. 269, p. 359 and *K.S.*, p. 381).

9 See above, pp. 8ff.

10 *Stern*, I, *Einleitung*, pp. 12–15.

11 Ibid., p. 26; see also *Briefe*, no. 307, p. 399.

12 'Vertauschte Fronten' (1929), *K.S.*, pp. 355–6.

13 *Stern*, I, p. 69.

14 *Briefe*, no. 31, p. 40.

15 Ibid., no. 40, p. 59.

16 The relevant documents are to be found in *Judaism Despite*

Christianity, ed. Eugen Rosenstock-Huessy, with essays by Alexander Altmann, Dorothy Emmet and H. Stahmer (Alabama, 1969).

17 This letter is not available in the published *Briefe*. It is here quoted from the English translation in N. Glatzer (ed.), *Franz Rosenzweig, His Life and Thought* (New York, 1961) pp. 94–8; cf. also H. Liebeschütz, *Von Simmel zu Rosenzweig* (Tübingen, 1970) pp. 152ff.

18 *Philosophy and Phenomenonological Research*, iii (1942–3) 53–77.

19 Cf. M. Schwarz, 'Religious Currents and General Culture', *Leo Baeck Year Book*, xvi (1971) pp. 14ff. See also the same author's 'Ha'Historiyosofiya Ha'Yehudit B'Mishnot Ranak Ve'Rosenzweig', *Safa, Mythos, Amanut* (Jerusalem, 1967) pp. 198ff.

20 'Das Neue Denken', *K.S.*, p. 374.

21 See M. Schwarz, 'Ha'Tfisa Ha'Realistit shel Ha'Mythos B'Mishnato shel F. Rosenzweig', *Safa*, pp. 185–9. Schelling was the first of Rosenzweig's guardian angels (*Briefe*, no. 221, p. 299). The others are given as Kant, Nietzsche, Feuerbach or Goethe (for references see Jacob Fleischmann, *Bayat Ha'Notzrut Ba' Mahashava Ha'Yehudit Mi'Mendelssohn ad Rosenzweig*, Jerusalem, 1964, p. 155).

22 'Fragmente aus dem Nachlass', *Schocken Almanach* 5699 (Berlin, 1938/9) p. 56; see also the criticism of Baeck and Brod in 'Apologetisches Denken', *K.S.*, pp. 31–42.

23 *Faust*, i, quoted 'Geist und Epochen der jüdischen Geschichte', *K.S.*, pp. 13–14.

24 Ibid., pp. 12–25.

25 *Briefe*, no. 316, p. 405.

26 See also above, p. 5.

27 *Stern*, ii, 2, p. 222.

28 *Briefe*, p. 676.

29 Cf. A. Altmann, 'Rosenzweig on History', in A. Altmann (ed.), *Between East and West* (London, 1958) p. 210.

30 *Stern*, iii, 2, p. 100.

31 Ibid., 1, p. 55.

32 'Die Bauleute', *K.S.*, p. 119.

33 Quoted ibid., p. 117. Rosenzweig later confessed that ignorance prevented him from doing full justice to the Law. He hoped to make good his neglect by further study (*Briefe*, no. 389, pp. 496–7).

34 *Stern*, iii, 2, pp. 103–4. But Rosenzweig also argued that the possibility of proselytisation must be held open (*Briefe*, p. 693).

35 See also below, p. 110.
36 Nohl, op. cit., p. 246.
37 *Stern*, III, 1, pp. 50–1. This is also argued at the metaphysico-spiritual level, ibid., 2, p. 112.
38 Ibid., pp. 49–50. It was this unattachment that led Rosenzweig to write jocularly of assimilated Jews living on their wits, as 'speculators, university teachers, journalists, bohemians, money-lenders . . .' *Briefe*, no. 159, p. 199.
39 Ibid., pp. 48–9.
40 Ibid., 2, p. 110.
41 Ibid., 1, pp. 56, 69, 71–2, 82; 2, p. 140.
42 *Stern*, III, 1, pp. 58–60.
43 Ibid., p. 61.
44 *Briefe*, no. 233, p. 316.
45 Ibid.
46 *Stern*, III, 3, pp. 187–8, 193–4.
47 'Das Neue Denken', *K.S.*, pp. 392–3.
48 *Briefe*, no. 59, p. 74.
49 *Stern*, III, 2, p. 102.
50 'Weltgeschichtliche Bedeutung der Bibel', *K.S.*, p. 126.
51 *Stern*, III, 1, pp. 87–91, 55.
52 Ibid., p. 91.
53 Ibid., pp. 104–5.
54 Ibid., p. 175.
55 *Briefe*, p. 671.
56 *Stern*, III, 1, p. 87; *Briefe*, p. 687.
57 *Stern*, III, 2, p. 102.
58 *Briefe*, no. 159, p. 202; *Stern*, III, 3, p. 197.
59 *Stern*, III, 3, 187.
60 *Guide to the Perplexed*, III, 27 (trans. S. Pines).
61 See also N. Rotenstreich, *Ha'Mahashava Ha'Yehudit ba'Et Ha'Hadasha*, II (Tel Aviv, 1950) p. 237; this criticism is further developed in E. Berkowitz, *Major Themes in Modern Philosophies of Judaism* (New York, 1974) pp. 47ff, and in D. Clawson, 'Rosenzweig on Judaism and Christianity', *Judaism*, XIX, no. 1 (1970) 90ff.
62 *Stern*, III, 1, p. 91.
63 See above, p. 109.
64 *Stern*, III, 1, p. 50.
65 'Geist und Epochen', *K.S.*, pp. 20ff.
66 *Stern*, III, pp. 50–1.
67 J. Fleischmann, 'Rosenzweig as a Critic of Zionism', *Conservative Judaism*, XXII, no. 1 (1967).

68 'Die Bauleute', *K.S.*, p. 120.
69 See Liebeschütz, op. cit., p. 154 and *Briefe*, no. 365, p. 476.
  This letter was written in February 1923.
70 *Stern*, III, 1, p. 56; See also 'Geist und Epochen', *K.S.*, pp. 23ff.

Conclusion

1 See above, p. 81.
2 *T.B. Sanhedrin*, 97b.
3 G. Scholem, *Judaica* (Frankfurt a. M., 1963 pp. 73ff. Note
  also Scholem's reference to 'the deep, dangerous and destructive
  dialectic inherent in the messianic idea . . .' (*Sabbatai Sevi, The
  Mystical Messiah 1626–1676*, London, 1973, preface, p. xii).
  There is a short critical discussion of these views by S. Schwarzschild in *Judaism*, x, no. 1 (1961) 72ff.
4 J. Petuchowski, 'Messianic Hope in Judaism', *Concilium*, VII/
  VIII, no. 10 (1974) 150–5.
5 *T.B. Shabbath*, 118a; *Sanhedrin*, 98a.
6 See above, p. 62.
7 *T.B. Sanhedrin*, 97a.
8 *T.B. Sanhedrin*, 98a.
9 Judith Shklar, 'Political Theory of Utopia', in F. E. Manuel
  (ed.), *Utopias and Utopian Thought* (London, 1973) p. 104; and
  the same author's *Men and Citizens* (Cambridge, 1969) p. 2.
10 *En passant*, here lies the explanation of the animus that the
  Jews have attracted, i.e. not in so far as they represent a mere
  enfant terrible or 'obstinate mute admonisher' à la Rosenzweig
  or serve as a mere reminder to others of their imperfections –
  this role could easily be tolerated – but in so far as the Jews
  follow a line of conduct, albeit with much backsliding and
  waywardness, congruent with a generally desired objective.
  Steiner's explanation of the animus (*In Bluebeard's Castle*,
  London, 1974) couched in terms of 'the insistence of the ideal'
  (p. 41) is equally defective and for the same reason.
11 See the discussion of this point in Horkheimer/Marcuse, 'Philosophie und kritische Theorie', *Zeitschrift für Sozialforschung*,
  VI, no. 3 (1937) 644ff.
12 *T.B. Shabbath*, 118b.
13 Op. cit., p. 112.

Select Bibliography

BABYLONIAN TALMUD : MIDRASH

Berakhoth	Sanhedrin
Shabbath	Makkoth
Pesahim	Avoda Zara
Ta'anith	Menahoth
Sotah	
Kiddushin	Midrash Rabbah
Baba Bathra	

GENERAL

Acton, Lord, *Essays on Freedom and Power*, ed. G. Himmelfarb (Boston, 1948).

Ahad Ha'am, *Igroth V, 1913–1919* (Jerusalem, Berlin, 1924).

Albert H., *Plädoyer für kritischen Rationalismus* (Munich, 1971).

Altmann, A., 'Gishot Shonot la'historiya ha'Yisraelit', *Yad Shaul*, ed. Weinberg and Biberfeld (Tel Aviv, 1953).

Baeck, Leo, *Aus drei Jahrtausenden* (Tübingen, 1958).

Baron, S. W., *A Social and Religious History of the Jews*, 2nd ed. (New York, 1952).

Berkowitz, E., *Major Themes in Modern Philosophies of Judaism* (New York, 1974).

Bloch, Marc., *Apologie pour l'histoire* (Paris, 1949).

Cohen, H., *Jüdische Schriften*, 3 vols (Berlin, 1924).

—— *Religion der Vernunft aus den Quellen des Judentums* (Leipzig, 1919).

Cohen, Morris, 'Philosophies of Jewish History', *Jewish Social Studies*, I, no. 1 (1939).

Elon, M., *Ha'Mishpat Ha'Ivri*, 3 vols (Jerusalem, 1973).

Fackenheim, E., *Metaphysics and Historicity* (Milwaukee, 1961).

Ginzberg, L., *Legends of the Jews*, 7 vols (New York, 1909–38).

Herr, M. D., 'Role of the Halacha in the Shaping of Jewish History', *Contemporary Thinking in Israel*, I (Jerusalem, 1973).

Horkheimer, M. and Marcuse, H., 'Philosophie und kritische Theorie', *Zeitschrift für Sozialforschung*, VI, no. 3 (1937).

Jews of Czechoslovakia, The II (Philadelphia, 1971).

Katz, B.-Z., *Rabbanut, Hasidut, Haskala,* 2 vols (Jerusalem, 1956, 1958).

Klempt, A., *Die Säkularisierung der universalhistorischen Auffassung im 16 and 17 Jahrhundert* (Göttingen, 1960).

Langmuir, Gavin, 'Majority History and Post-Biblical Jews', *Journal of the History of Ideas*, vol. 27 (1966).

Lazar, L., *Die Geschichtsauffassung der Propheten im Verhältnis zur Geschichtsphilosophie des Idealismus der Gegenwart* (Lodz, 1935).

Lestchinsky, J., 'Do Jews Learn From History?', *Jewish Journal of Sociology*, v, no. 2.

Macaulay, T. B., 'Civil Disabilities of the Jews', *Edinburgh Review*, 1831.

Meyer, M., *Origins of the Modern Jew* (Wayne State U.P., 1967).

Moore, G. F., 'Christian Writers on Judaism', *Harvard Theological Review*, XIV (1921).

Moryson, Fynes, *Shakespeare's Europe*, ed. Charles Hughes (New York, 1967).

Nietzsche, F., *Werke* I: *Vom Nutzen und Nachteil der Historie für das Leben* (Munich, 1954).

Plumb, J. H., *The Death of the Past* (London, 1969).

Pocock, J. G. A., *Politics, Language and Time* (London, 1972).

Raphael, F., 'Weber and Judaism', *Leo Baeck Year Book*, XVIII (1973).

Ruether, Rosemary, *Faith and Fratricide* (London, 1975).

Shklar, J., 'Political Theory of Utopia', in F. E. Manuel (ed.), *Utopias and Utopian Thought* (London, 1973).

Steiner, G., *In Bluebeard's Castle* (London, 1974).

Toynbee, A., *A Study of History* (Oxford U.P., 1933).

Verete, M., 'The Restoration of the Jews in English Protestant Thought 1790–1840', *Middle Eastern Studies* (Jan. 1972).

Vico, G., *Autobiography*, ed. and trans. Fisch and Bergin (New York, 1963).

Weber, M., *Gesammelte Aufsätze zur Religionssoziologie*, III (Tübingen, 1923).

—— *Gesammelte Aufsätze zur Wissenschaftslehre* (Tübingen, 1951).

Werblowsky, R. J., 'Judaism, or the Religion of Israel', in R. C. Zaehner (ed.), *The Concise Encyclopaedia of Living Faiths* (London, 1959).

Wilhelm, K., 'Zur Einführung in die Wissenschaft des Judentums', in K. Wilhelm (ed.), *Wissenschaft des Judentums im deutschen Sprachbereich*, I (Tübingen, 1966).

Wolfsberg, Y., *Mkoma shel ha'Historiya ba'filosofiya ha'datit* (Sinai, 1938) I, pt 4.

HISTORICAL

Abrabanel, Don Isaac, *Ma'ayenei Ha'Yeshuah* (Stettin, 1860).

—— *Ateret Zekenim* (Warsaw, 1894).

—— *Mashmia Yeshuah* (Offenbach, 1767).

—— *Yeshuot Meshiho* (Königsberg, 1861).

Agus, A. I., *Al Historiografiya shel Yisrael ba'golah*, S. K. Mirsky Jubilee Volume, ed. Bernstein and Churgin (New York, 1958).

Altmann, A., 'Rosenzweig on History', in A. Altmann (ed.), *Between East and West* (London, 1958).

—— *Moses Mendelssohn* (London, 1973).

Auerbach, Sh., 'Shimon Dubnovs Shtellung tzu Yiddish un Hebräisch', in A. Steinberg (ed.), *Simon Dubnow and his Work* (World Jewish Congress, Paris, 1963).

Baer, I., 'Eine jüdische Messiasprophetie auf das Jahr 1186 und der dritte Kreuzzug and II, Messianische Bewegungen um 1186, *Monatsschrift für die Geschichte und Wissenschaft des Judentums*, Hefte 3/4, 5/6 (1926).

—— Galut (Berlin, 1936).

—— 'Le'Berur ha'Matzav shel ha'limudim ha'historiim etzlenu', *Sefer Magnes* (Jerusalem, 1938).

—— *Toldoth Ha'Yehudim bi'Sefarad Ha'Notzrit* 2nd ed. (Tel Aviv, 1965).

——'Don Yitzhak Abrabanel Ve'Yahso el Baiyot Ha'Historiya Ve'Ha'Medina', *Tarbitz*, VIII, nos. 3–4 (Jerusalem, 1937).

Bamberger, F., 'Zunz's Conception of History', *Proceedings of the American Academy for Jewish Research*, XI (1941).

Bar Hiyya, R. Abraham, *Megilat Ha'Megaleh*, ed. A. Poznanski, revised and with an introduction by Julius Guttman (Berlin, 1924).

Baron, S. W., 'Azariah dei Rossi's Historical Method', *History and Jewish Historians* (Philadelphia, 1964).

Barzilay, I., *Shlomo Yehudah Rapaport* (Israel, 1969).

Bazak, H., 'Ma'aseh Avoth Siman le'banim be'Perush Ha'Ramban', *Ha'Ma'ayan*, xv, no. 3 (1975).

Ben-Sasson, H. H., 'Musagim u'metziut ba'historiya ha'yehudit b'shilhe ymei ha'beinayim', *Tarbitz*, XXIX (1959–60).

—— *Hagut Ve'Hanhaga* (Jerusalem, 1959).

150 *Select Bibliography*

—— *Galut u'Geulah b'eynav shel dor Golé Sepharad,* I. Baer Jubilee Volume (Jerusalem, 1960).

—— 'L'Magamot ha'Kronografiya ha'Yehudit shel ymei ha'beinayim u'Bayoteha', *Historiyonim v'askolot historiyot* (Jerusalem, 1962).

—— 'The Reformation in Contemporary Jewish Eyes', *Proceedings of Israel Academy of Sciences and Humanities,* iv, no. 12 (Jerusalem, 1970).

—— 'Jews and Christian Sectarians', *Viator,* no. 4 (1973).

—— *Al Tod'atenu Ha'Historit* (Molad, 1975) 33–4.

Berger, Israel, *Esser Tsahtsahot* (Piotrkow, 1910).

Bernfeld, S., 'Dorshei Reshumot', *Ha'Shiloah,* ii (Apr–Sept 1899).

—— *Bnei Aliya* (Tel Aviv, 1931).

—— *Mendelssohns Wirken im Judentum, Mendelssohn–zur 200-jährigen Wiederkehr seines Geburtstages, Encyclopaedia Judaica* (Berlin, 1929).

Bickermann, E., 'La Chaîne de la tradition pharisienne', *Revue Biblique,* lix, (1952).

Bloch, P., *Heinrich Graetz, A Memoir* (London, 1898).

Boehlich, W. (ed.), *Der Berliner Antisemitismusstreit* (Frankfurt a.M., 1965).

Breuer, M., 'Magamotav shel Zemach David', *Ha'Ma'ayan,* v, no. 2 (1965).

—— 'Kavim l'demuto shel R. David Gans', *Annual of the University of Bar Ilan,* xi (1973).

Cahana, A., *Sifrut Ha'Historiya Ha'Yisraelit,* 2 vols (Warsaw, 1922).

Cassirer, E., *Die Idee der Religion bei Lessing und Mendelssohn,* Festgabe zum zehnjährigen Bestehen der Akademie für die Wissenschaft des Judentums 1919–1929 (Berlin, 1929).

Chazan, R., 'R. Ephraim of Bonn's Sefer Zekhira', *Revue des Etudes Juives,* cxxxii (Jan–June 1973).

Childs, B. S., *Memory and Tradition in Israel,* Studies in Biblical Theology, no. 37 (London, 1962).

Clawson, D., 'Rosenzweig on Judaism and Christianity', *Judaism,* xix, no. 7 (1970).

Cohen, G. D., 'Messianic Postures of Ashkenazim and Sephardim', Leo Baeck Memorial Lecture 9, (New York, 1967).

Davis, M., 'Jewry East and West–The Correspondence of I. Friedländer and S. Dubnow', *Yivo Annual,* ix (New York, 1954).

Dubnow, S., *Die Weltgeschichte des jüdischen Volks,* German trans., 10 vols (Berlin, 1925–9).

—— *Jewish History – An Essay in the Philosophy of History,* English trans. (London, 1903).

——*Mein Leben*, ed. E. Hurwicz (Berlin, 1937).

—— (ed.), *Pinkas Ha'Medina* (repr. Jerusalem, 1969).

Dubnowá-Erlikh, S., *Zhizn i Tvorchestvo S.M.Dubnova* (New York, 1950).

Elbaum, J., 'R. Judah Loew of Prague and his Attitude to the Aggadah', *Scripta Hierosolymitana*, xxii (1971).

Elbogen, I., *Abraham ibn Daud als Geschichtsschreiber, Festschrift für Jakob Guttman* (Leipzig, 1915).

—— 'Von Graetz bis Dubnow', *Dubnow Festschrift*, ed. J. Meisl, I. Elbogen, M. Wischnitzer (Berlin, 1930).

Emden, R. Jacob, *Megilat Sefer*, ed. D. Cahana (Warsaw, 1896).

Ephraim, R., of Bonn, *Sefer Zekhira*, ed. A. M. Habermann (Jerusalem, 1970).

Ettinger, S. (ed.), *Graetz, Darkhe Ha'Historiya Ha'Yehudit*, with a biographical introduction by R. Michael (Jerusalem, 1969).

Fleischmann, J., *Bayat Ha'Notzrut Ba'Mahashava Ha'Yehudit Mi'Mendelssohn ad Rosenzweig* (Jerusalem, 1964).

—— 'Rosenzweig as a Critic of Zionism', *Conservative Judaism*, xxii, no. 1 (1967).

Frankel, Z., 'Über den Lapidarstil der talmudischen Historik', *MGWJ*, i (1852).

Funkenstein, A., 'Gesetz und Geschichte; Zur historisierenden Hermeneutik bei Moses Maimonides und Thomas von Aquin', *Viator*, 1 (1970).

Gans, David, *Zemach David* (Lemberg, 1847).

—— *Zemach David*, ed. Hominer (Jerusalem, 1966).

Geiger, A., *Nachgelassene Schriften* ii, ed. L. Geiger (Berlin, 1875).

Geis, R. R., 'Das Geschichtsbild des Talmud', *Saeculum*, vi (1955).

Glatzer, N., *Untersuchungen zur Geschichtslehre der Tannaiten* (Berlin, 1932).

—— 'The Beginnings of Modern Jewish Studies', A. Altmann (ed.), *Studies in Nineteenth-Century Jewish Intellectual History* (Cambridge, Mass., 1964).

—— 'The Attitude towards Rome in Third-Century Judaism', *Politische Ordnung und Menschliche Existenz – Festgabe für E. Voegelin* (Munich, 1962).

—— 'Klalim b'tfisat-ha'historiya shel Zunz', *Zion*, xxi (1961).

—— *Franz Rosenzweig, His Life and Thought* (New York, 1961).

Gottesdiener, A., 'Ha'Ari she b'Hochmei Prag', *Azkarah le' Ha'rav Kuk*, ed. J. L. Fischmann, iv (Jerusalem, 1937).

Graetz, H., *Die Konstruktion der jüdischen Geschichte* (repr. Berlin, 1936).

F

—— *Geschichte der Juden von den ältesten Zeiten bis zur Gegenwart*, 11 vols, (Leipzig, 1853ff).

—— 'Die Verjüngung des jüdischen Stammes', *Jahrbuch für Israeliten*, n.s., vol. x, Vienna (1864).

——'Entwicklungsstadien des Messiasglaubens', ibid., vol. xi, Vienna (1865).

—— *Briefwechsel einer englischen Dame über Judentum und Semitismus* (Stuttgart, 1883).

—— *Historic Parallels in Jewish History*, a discourse delivered at the Anglo-Jewish Historical Exhibition, 16 June, 1887 (London, 1887).

—— 'The Significance of Judaism for Present and Future', *Jewish Quarterly Review*, 1 (Oct. 1888).

Gross, B., *Le Messianisme Juif: Etudes Maharaliennes II* (Paris, 1969).

Grunfeld, Dr I. (ed.), *Judaism Eternal*, 2 vols (London, 1956).

Guttman, Jakob, *Die religionsphilosophischen Lehren des Isaak Abravanel* (Breslau, 1916).

Halperin, R. Yehiel, *Seder Ha'Dorot* (repr. Jerusalem, 1956).

Herlitz, G., 'Three Jewish Historians', *Yearbook of the Leo Baeck Institute*, ix (London, 1964).

Heschel, A., *Don Yizchak Abrabanel* (Berlin, 1937).

Hess, M., *Rom und Jerusalem* (Leipzig, 1862).

—— *Die Europäische Triarchie* (Leipzig, 1841).

Hirsch, S. R., *Gesammelte Schriften* (Frankfurt a.M., 1908).

Holdheim, S., *Das Ceremonialgesetz im Messiasreich* (Schwerin, 1845).

Horwitz, R., 'Tfisat Ha'Historiya Ha'Yehudit b'Mahashevet Rosenzweig', *Proceedings of the American Academy for Jewish Research*, New York (1969).

—— 'Judaism despite Christianity', *Judaism*, xxiv, no. 3 (1975).

—— 'Franz Rosenzweig's unpublished writings', *Journal of Jewish Studies*, xx, nos 1–4 (1969).

Ibn Daud, R. Abraham, *Sefer Ha'Qabbalah*, ed. G. D. Cohen (Philadelphia, 1967; London, 1969).

Ibn Verga, R. Solomon, *Shevet Yehudah*, ed. A. Shohat (Jerusalem, 1947).

Ibn Yahya, Gedaliah, *Shalshelet Ha'Kabbalah* (Warsaw, 1877).

Igreth R. Sherira Gaon, ed. Aaron Hyman (London, 1910).

Jost, I. M., *Geschichte des Judentums und Seiner Secten* (Leipzig, 1859).

Kalonymos, R. Judah ben, *Yehuse Tannaim ve'Amoraim*, ed. R.J.L. Ha'Cohen Maimon (Jerusalem, 1963).

Kaplan, S., *Das Geschichtsproblem in der Philosophie Hermann Cohens* (Berlin, 1930).

Kariv, A. (ed.), *Kitve Maharal MiPrag*, 2 vols (Jerusalem, 1972).

Katsh, A., 'Nachman Krochmal and the German Idealists', *Jewish Social Studies*, VIII (1946).

Kaufman, D., *Gesammelte Schriften*, ed. M. Brann (Frankfurt a.M., 1908–15).

Kaupp, P., 'Toynbee and the Jews', *Weiner Library Bulletin*, XXI, no. 1 (winter 1966–7).

Kobler, F., *The Vision Was There* (London, 1956).

Kohn, J., *Soziologische Einführungsskizze in die Geschichtsschreibung des Judentums in der Çeskoslovakischen Republik*, Jahrbuch der Gesellschaft für die Geschichte der Juden in der Çeskoslovakischen Republik, II (1930).

Krochmal, R. Nahman, *Kitve*, ed. S. Rawidowicz (London, 1961).

Lachover, P., *Al Gvul Ha'Yashan Ve'He'Hadash* (Jerusalem, 1951).

Landau, J. L., *Nahman Krochmal – ein Hegelianer* (Berlin, 1904).

Lavrov, P., *Istoricheskie Pisma* (St Petersburg, 1906).

Liebeschütz, H., 'Treitschke und Mommsen', *Leo Baeck Year Book*, VII (1962).

—— 'Jewish Thought and its German Background', *Year Book of the Leo Baeck Institute*, I (London, 1956).

—— *Das Judentum im deutschen Geschichtsbild von Hegel bis Max Weber* (Tübingen, 1967).

—— *Von Simmel zu Rosenzweig* (Tübingen, 1970).

Loeb, I., 'Le folk-lore juif dans la chronique du Schébet Iehuda d'Ibn Verga', *Revue des Etudes juives*, XXXIV (1892).

Loew, R. Judah of Prague, *Netzah Israel* (London, 1960).

—— *Be'er Ha'Golah* (Jerusalem, 1971).

—— *Tifereth Israel* (Jerusalem, 1970).

—— *Or Hadash* (Jerusalem, 1944).

—— *Gevurot Ha'Shem* (Jerusalem, 1971).

—— *Netivot Olam* (Warsaw, 1884).

Löwith, K., 'M. Heidegger and F. Rosenzweig', *Philosophy and Phenomenological Research*, III (1942–3).

Luzzatto, S. D., *Igrot Shadal*, V, VII, ed. Graeber (Cracow, 1884).

Maimon, S., *Autobiography*, English trans. (London, 1957).

Maimonides, Moses, *Mishneh Torah*.

—— *Commentary on the Mishnah*.

—— *Moreh Nevukhim*.

Mauskopf, A., *The Religious Philosophy of the Maharal of Prague*, 2nd ed. (New York, 1966).

Meisl, J., *Graetz, eine Würdigung* (Berlin, 1917).

Mendelssohn, M., *Gesammelte Schriften* v, Briefe, ed. G. B. Mendelssohn (Leipzig, 1844).

—— *Jerusalem.*

Mevorah, B., 'The Problem of the Messiah in the Emancipation and Reform Controversies 1781–1819', unpublished Ph.D. thesis (Jerusalem, 1966).

—— *Napoleon u'tekufato* (Jerusalem, 1968).

Meyer, M., 'Jewish Religious Reform and Wissenschaft des Judentums', *Yearbook of the Leo Baeck Institute*, xvi (London, 1971).

—— (ed.), *Ideas of Jewish History* (New York, 1974).

—— 'Where Does Modern Jewish History Begin?' *Judaism*, xxiv, no. 3 (1975).

Michael, R., 'Graetz und Hess', *Year Book of the Leo Baeck Institute*, ix (1964).

Momigliano, A., 'Time in Ancient Historiography', *History and Theory*, Beiheft 6 (1966).

Nahman, R. Moses ben, *Torat Ha'Shem Temima*, ed. A. Jellinek (Leipzig, 1853).

Néher, A., *Le Puits de l'Exil* (Paris, 1966).

—— *David Gans* (Paris, 1974).

Netanyahu, B., *Don Isaac Abrabanel* (Philadelphia, 1968).

Neubauer, A. N., *Medieval Jewish Chronicles* (repr. Amsterdam, 1970).

Neuman, A. A. *The Shebet Yehudah and Sixteenth-Century Historiography*, Louis Ginzberg Jubilee Volume, English Section (New York, 1945).

Neusner, J., 'Religious Uses of History', *History and Theory*, v, no. 2 (1966).

—— 'Review Essay – Ideas of Jewish History', ibid., xiv, no. 2 (1975).

Nohl, H. (ed.), *Hegels theologische Jugendschriften* (Tübingen, 1907).

Orlinsky, H. M., 'On Toynbee's Use of the Term Syriac for One of His Societies', *In the Time of Harvest, Essays in Honour of Abba Hillel Silver* (New York, 1963).

Pesikta de Rav Kahana, ed. S. Buber (Lyck, 1868).

Petuchowski, J., 'Messianic Hope in Judaism', *Concilium* vii/viii, no. 10 (1974).

Pinson, K. (ed.), *Nationalism and History. Essays on Old and New Judaism by S. Dubnow* (Philadelphia, 1958).

Publications of the American Jewish Historical Society, II, no. 27 (1920).

Rabin, I., 'Stoff und Idee in der jüdischen Geschichtsschreibung', *Dubnow Festschrift*, ed. Elbogen, Meisl, Wischnitzer (Berlin, 1930).

Radday, Y., 'Does Archaeology contribute to a better understanding of Scripture?', *Dispersion and Unity*, 19/20 (1973).

Rappoport, R. Solomon Judah, 'R. Yehiel of Rome', *Bikkurei Ha'Ittim*, x (1829).

Rawidowicz, S. (ed.), *Sefer Dubnow* (London, Jerusalem, 1954), articles by R. Mahler, J. Meisl, J. Lestchinsky, M. Wischnitzer.

—— *Iyunim*, II (Jerusalem, 1971).

—— 'Nachman Krochmal als Historiker', *Dubnow Festschrift* (Berlin, 1930).

—— 'Ranak b'tor hoker u'mvaker', *Ha'Shiloach*, XLII, no. 2, 3 (1924).

—— 'War Nachman Krochmal Hegelianer?', *Hebrew Union College Annual*, VI, Cincinnati (1928).

Reissner, H. G., 'Rebellious Dilemma', *Year Book of the Leo Baeck Institute*, II (London, 1957).

Rohr, J., 'Die Prophetie im letzten Jahrhundert vor der Reformation als Geschichtsquelle und Geschichtsfaktor', *Historisches Jahrbuch der Görresgesellschaft*, XIX (Munich 1898).

Rosenstock-Huessy, E. (ed.), *Judaism Despite Christianity* (Alabama U.P., 1969).

Rosenthal, Erwin I. J., 'Don Isaac Abravanel : Financier, Statesman and Scholar', *Bulletin of the John Rylands Library* (Manchester, 1937).

—— 'Hermann Cohen and Heinrich Graetz', *S.W. Baron Jubilee Volume*, II (Jerusalem, 1974).

Rosenzweig, F., *Der Stern der Erlösung* (repr. Heidelberg, 1954).

—— *Briefe* (Berlin, 1935).

—— *Kleinere Schriften* (Berlin, 1937).

—— *Fragmente aus dem Nachlass*, Schocken Almanach, 5699 (Berlin, 1938–9).

Rossi, Azariah dei, *Me'or Eynayim*, 3 vols, ed. D. Cassel (Vilna, 1866).

Rotenstreich, N., 'T'fisto Ha'Historit shel Ranak', *Zion*, VII (Apr–July 1942).

—— 'Nisyono shel Graetz ba'filosifiya shel ha'historiya', *Zion*, VIII, no. 1 (1943).

—— 'Hegel's Image of Judaism', *Jewish Social Studies*, XV, no. 1 (Jan 1953).

—— *The Recurring Pattern* (London, 1963).

—— *Tradition and Reality* (New York, 1972).

—— *Ha'Mahashava Ha'Yehudit ba'Et Ha'Hadasha*, 2 vols (Tel Aviv, 1945–50).

Rudavsky, D., 'S.D. Luzzatto and Neo-Orthodoxy', *Tradition*, VII, no. 3 (1965).

Sarachek, J., *The Doctrine of the Messiah in Medieval Jewish Literature*, 2nd ed. (New York, 1968).

Scholem, G., *Major Trends in Jewish Mysticism* (London, New York, 1961).

—— *Sabbatai Sevi, The Mystical Messiah 1626–1676* (London, Princeton, 1973).

—— *Judaica* (Frankfurt a.M., 1963).

Schorsch, I., 'The Philosophy of History of Nachman Krochmal', *Judaism*, x, no. 3 (1961).

—— (trans. and ed.), *Heinrich Graetz, The Structure of Jewish History and other essays* (New York, 1975).

Schreiber, E., *Graetzens Geschichtsbauerei* (Berlin, 1881).

Schwarz, M., 'Ha'Historiyosofiya Ha'Yehudit B'Mishnot Ranak Ve'Rosenzweig' *Safa, Mythos, Amanut* (Jerusalem, 1967).

—— 'Mkomo shel Franz Rosenzweig ba'filosofiya shel ha'Yahadut', introduction to Hebrew translation of *Der Stern der Erlösung* (Jerusalem, 1970).

—— 'Religious Currents and General Culture', *Leo Baeck Year Book*, xvi (1971).

Schwarzschild, S., 'Two Modern Jewish Philosophers of History, Nahman Krochmal and Hermann Cohen', unpublished Ph.D thesis (Hebrew Union College, Cincinnati, 1955).

—— *Franz Rosenzweig, Guide of Reversioners* (London, 1961).

Schweid, E., 'Ha'Tsionut ve'zikta le'tod'at he'avar ha'yehudi', *Hakarat He'Avar* (Jerusalem, 1969).

Seder Eliyahu Rabbah, ed. M. Friedmann (Vienna, 1904).

Seder Olam Rabbah, ed. B. Ratner (Vilna, 1897).

Seder Olam Zuta, ed. M. Grossberg (London, 1910).

Seder Tannaim Ve'Amoraim, ed. M. Grossberg (London, 1910).

Sedinova, J., 'Non-Jewish Sources in "The Chronicle" by David Gans'; 'Czech history as reflected in the historical work by David Gans', *Judaica Bohemiae*, viii, nos. 1, 2 (Prague, 1972).

Segal, M., 'R. Yitzhak Abrabanel b'Tor Parshan Ha'Mikrah', *Tarbitz*, viii, nos. 3–4 (Jerusalem, 1934).

Shmueli, E., *Don Yitzchak Abrabanel ve'Gerush Sepharad* (Jerusalem, 1963).

Shulvass, M., *Hayyei Ha'Yehudim B'Italiya Bi'Tkufat Ha'Renaissance* (New York, 1955).

—— *Ha'Yedia b'Historiya ve'ha'Sifrut ha'historit bi'Tkhum ha'Tarbut shel ha'Yahadut ha'Ashkenazit bi'ymei ha'beinayim*, Sefer Ha'Yovel le' R. H. Albeck (Jerusalem, 1963).

Siev, A., *Rabbenu Moshe Isserlis* (New York, 1972).

Silberner, E., *Moses Hess* (Leiden, 1966).

Sofer, P., 'Sergei Bershadsky', *He'Avar*, xx (1973).

Southern, R. W., 'Aspects of the European tradition of historical writing : 2. Hugh of St. Victor and the idea of historical development', *Transactions of the Royal Historical Society*, 5th series, xxi (1971).

Spanier, A., *Die Toseftaperiode in der tannaitischen Literatur* (Berlin, 1936).

Steinberg, A., 'Die weltanschaulichen Voraussetzungen der jüdischen Geschichtsschreibung', *Festschrift zu Dubnows 70tem Geburtstag*, ed. J. Meisl, I. Elbogen, M. Wischnitzer (Berlin, 1930).

Steinherz, S., 'Sage und Geschichte', *JGGJ in der Ceskoslowakischen Republik*, ix (1938).

Steinschneider, M., *Die Geschichtsliteratur der Juden* (Frankfurt, 1905).

Stern, S., *Josel of Rosheim* (Philadelphia, 1965).

Stitskin, L., *Judaism as a Philosophy* (New York, 1960).

Strauss, L., 'On Abravanel's Philosophical Tendency and Political Teachings', *Isaac Abravanel*, ed. J. B. Trend and H. Loewe (Cambridge U.P., 1937).

Taubes, J., 'Krochmal and Modern Historicism', *Judaism*, xii, no. 2 (1963).

Tcherikower, Elias, 'Jewish Martyrology and Jewish Historiography', *Yivo Annual of Jewish Social Science*, i (New York, 1946).

Urbach, E. E., *Baalei Ha'Tosafot* (Jerusalem, 1955).

Voos, Julius, 'David Reuveni und Salomo Molcho', inaugural dissertation, Bonn, 1933.

Weinryb, B. D., *Reappraisals in Jewish History*, S. W. Baron Jubilee Volume, ii (Jerusalem, 1974).

Weisl, N. H., *Divrei Shalom Ve'Emeth*.

Wiener, M., 'Aufriss einer jüdischen Theologie', *Hebrew Union College Annual*, xviii (1943–4).

Wigoder, G. (ed. and trans.), *The Meditation of the Sad Soul* (London, 1969).

Wolff, P., 'The 1391 Pogrom in Spain – Social Crisis or not?', *Past and Present*, no. 50 (Feb. 1971).

Zacuto, R. Abraham, *Sefer Yuhasin*, ed. H. Filipowski (Edinburgh, 1857).

Zunz, L., *Gesammelte Schriften*, 3 vols (Berlin, 1876).

—— *Literaturgeschichte der synagogalen Poesie* (Berlin, 1865).

—— *Toldoth R. Azariah min Ha'Edumim, Matzref la'Kessef*, ed. Isaac Ben-Yaakov, III (Vilna, 1865).

Index